INTERREGNA

INTERREGNA

John Pilson

HATJE
CANTZ

For Jack and Audrey

Graphic design: Christine Moog
Typeface: Univers
Paper: Galaxi Supermat 200 g/m^2
Binding: Verlagsbuchbinderei Dieringer, Gerlingen
Reproductions and printing: Dr. Cantz'sche Druckerei, Ostfildern

Published by
Hatje Cantz Verlag
Zeppelinstrasse 32
73760 Ostfildern
Germany
Tel. +49 711 4405-200
Fax +49 711 4405-220
www.hatjecantz.com

A special Collector's Edition is available. Please contact Hatje Cantz for more information.

Hatje Cantz books are available internationally at selected bookstores and from the following distribution partners:
USA/North America — D.A.P., Distributed Art Publishers, New York, www.artbook.com
UK — Art Books International, London, www.art-bks.com
Australia — Tower Books, Frenchs Forest (Sydney), www.towerbooks.com.au
France — Interart, Paris, www.interart.fr
Belgium — Exhibitions International, Leuven, www.exhibitionsinternational.be
Switzerland — Scheidegger, Affoltern am Albis, www.ava.ch

For Asia, Japan, South America, and Africa, as well as for general questions, please contact Hatje Cantz directly at sales@hatjecantz.de, or visit our homepage at www.hatjecantz.com for further information.

ISBN 978-3-7757-1898-1
Printed in Germany

Front cover: *Interregna (Grapefruit)*, detail, 1998–2000
Back cover: *Interregna (Monster)*, detail, 1998–2000

CONTENTS

FOREWORD

Between 1994 and 2000 I worked weekend and night shifts for an investment bank in Manhattan's Financial District. These photographs were taken during that time.

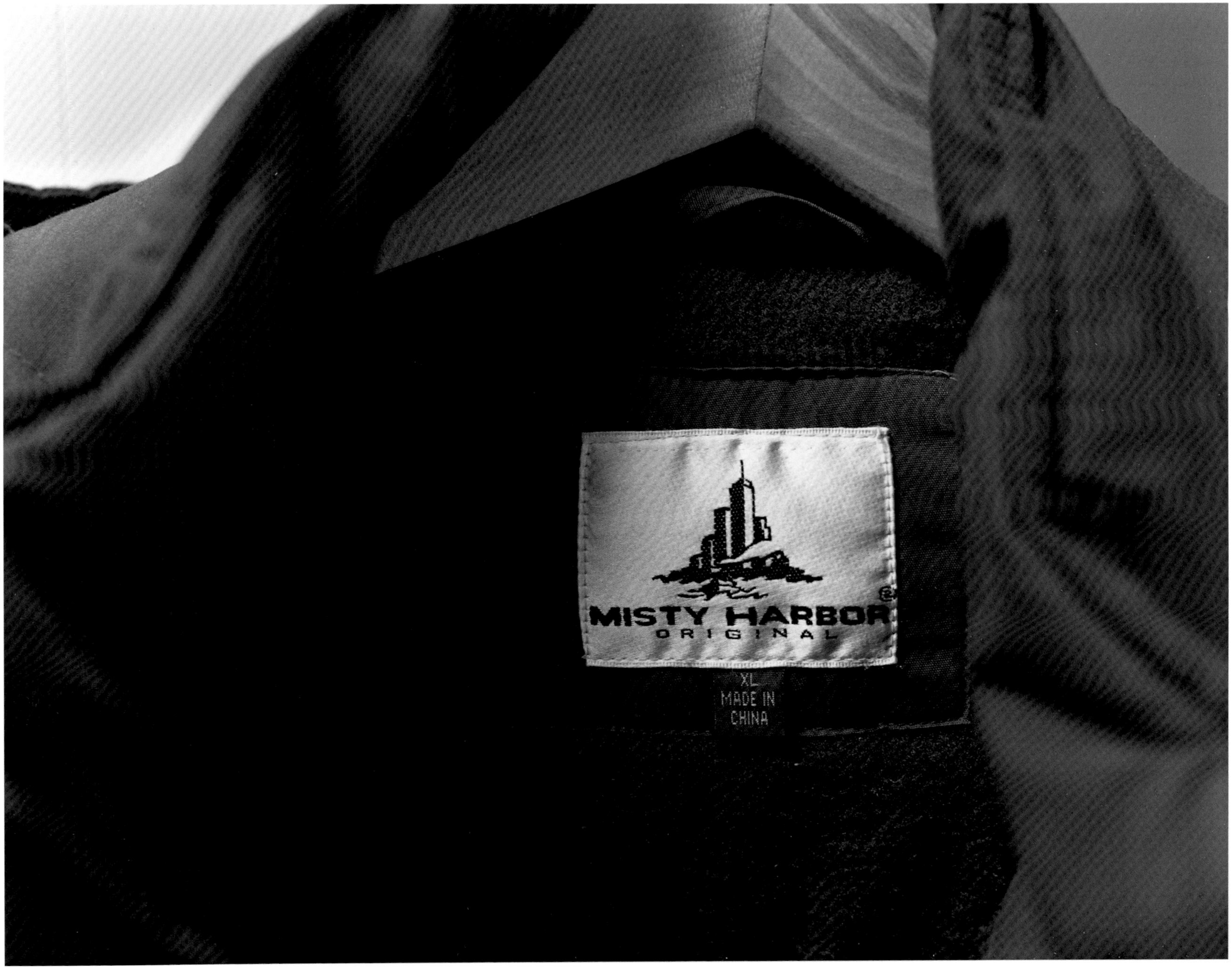
MISTY HARBOR®
ORIGINAL
XL
MADE IN
CHINA

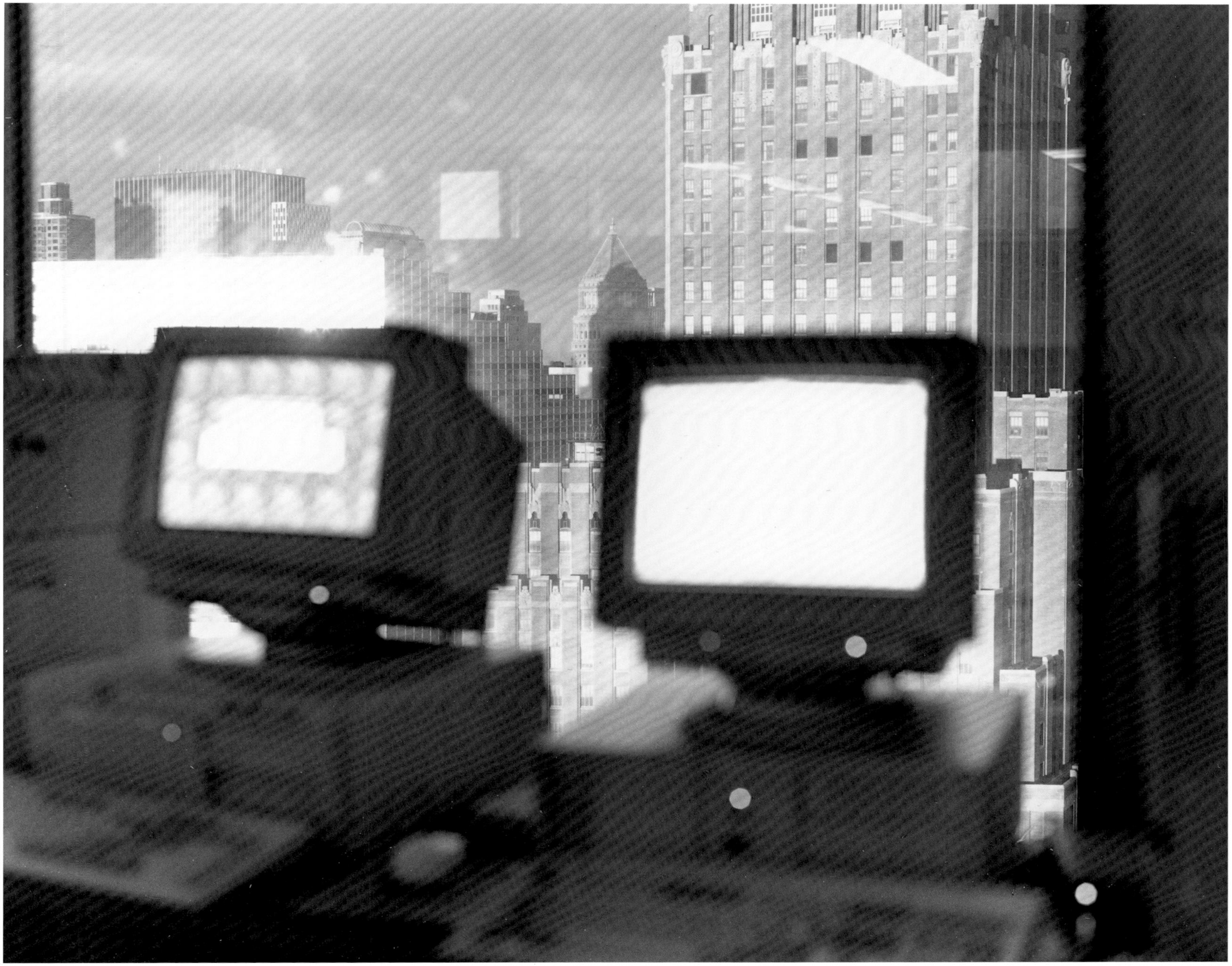

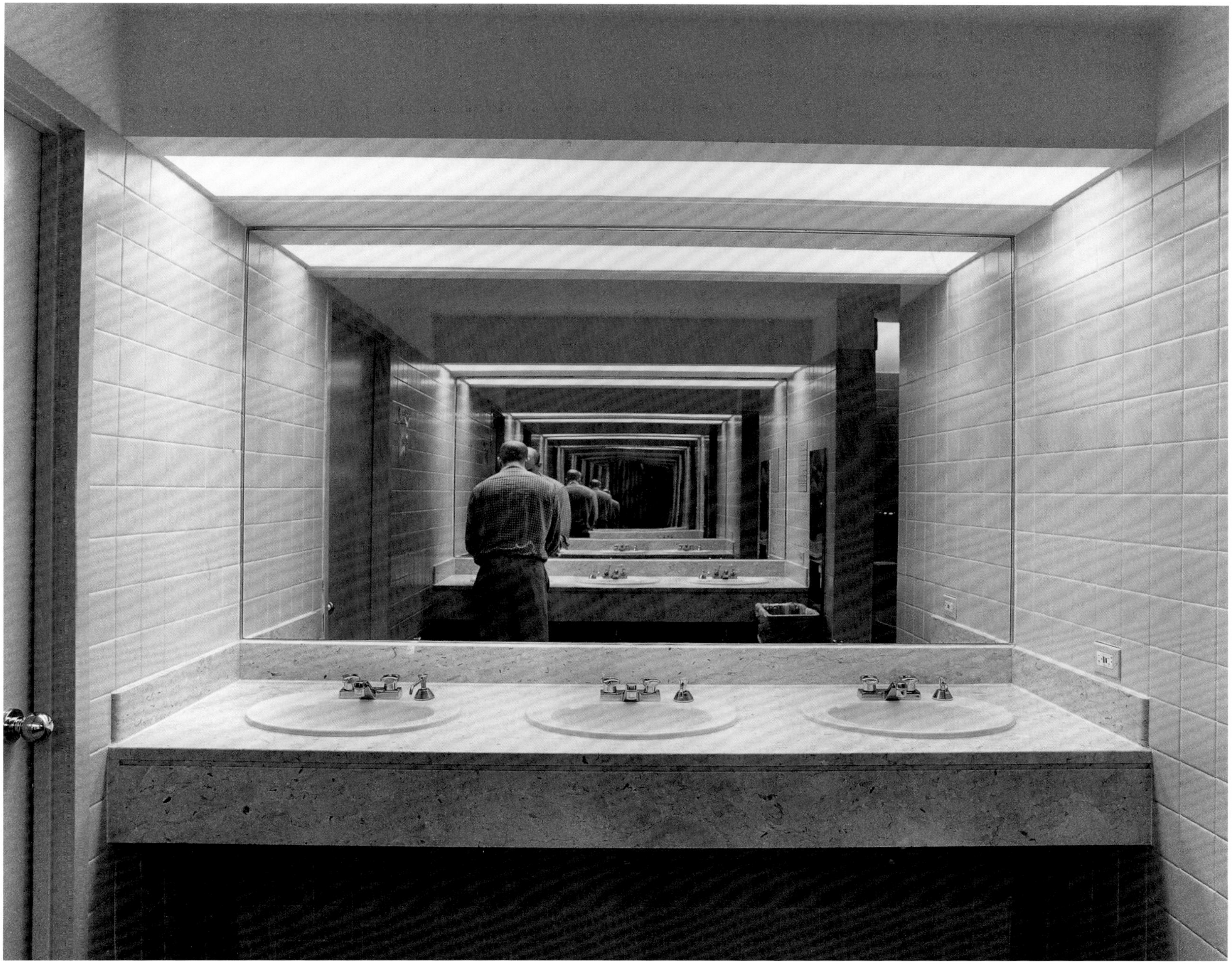

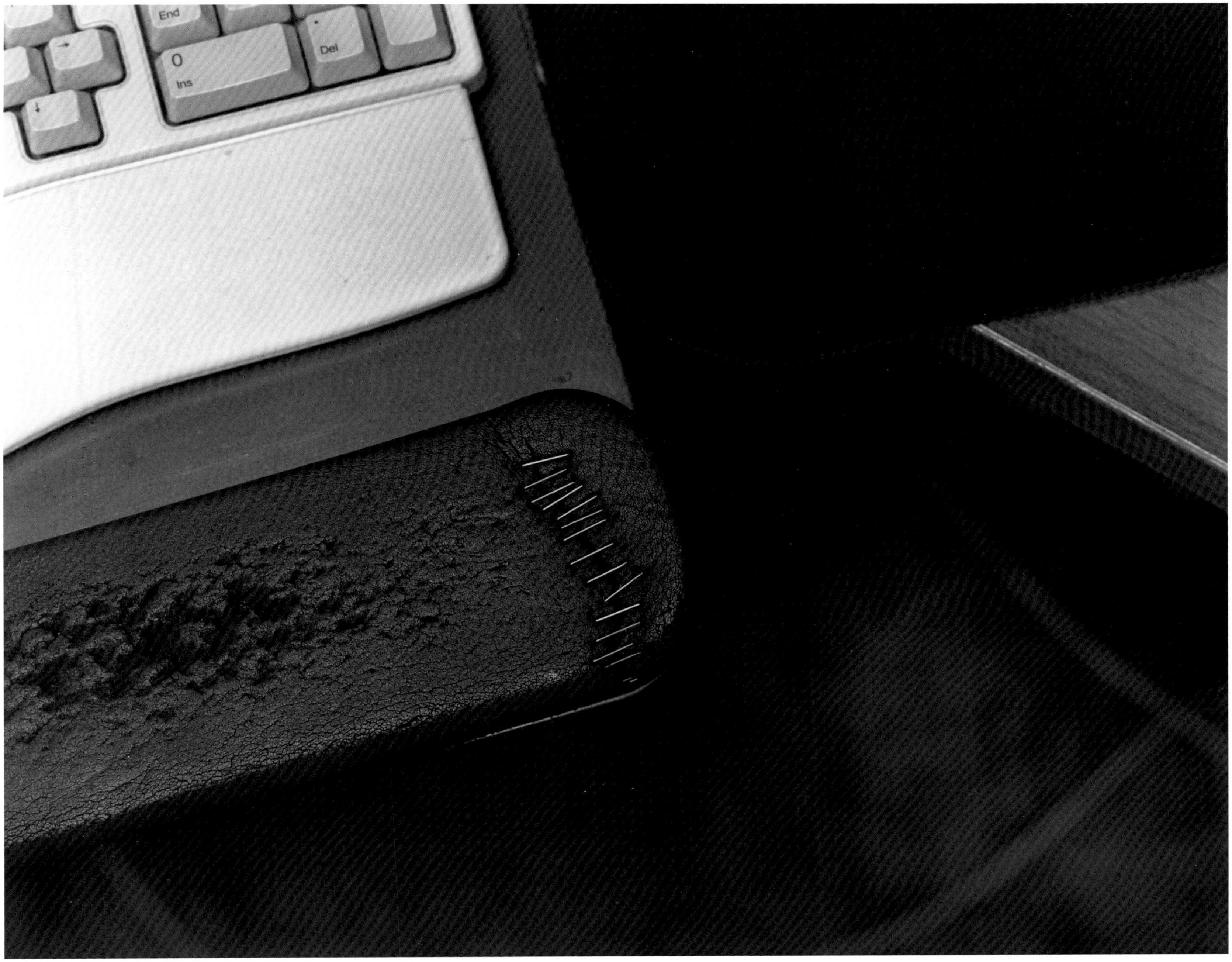
End
0
Ins
Del

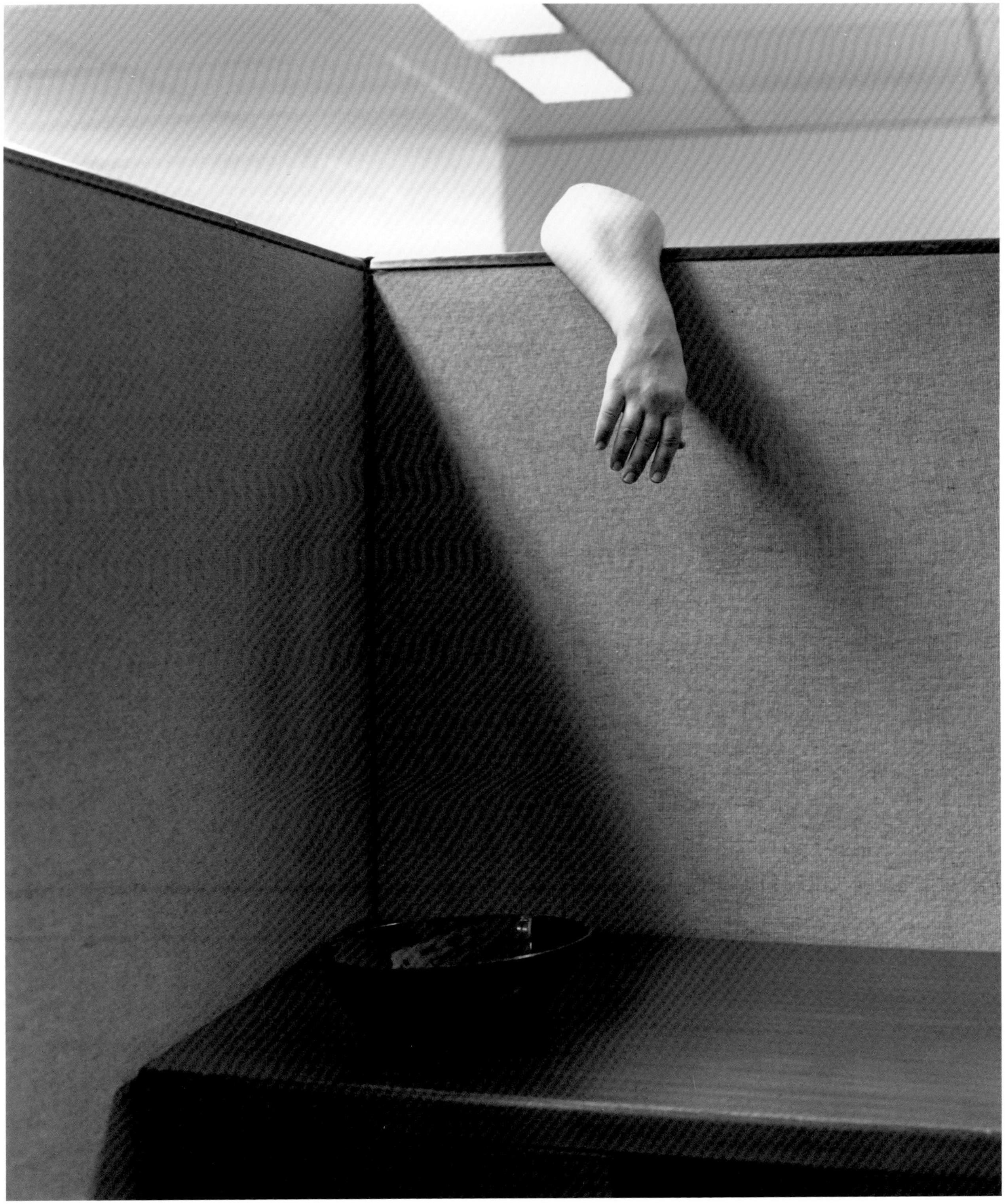

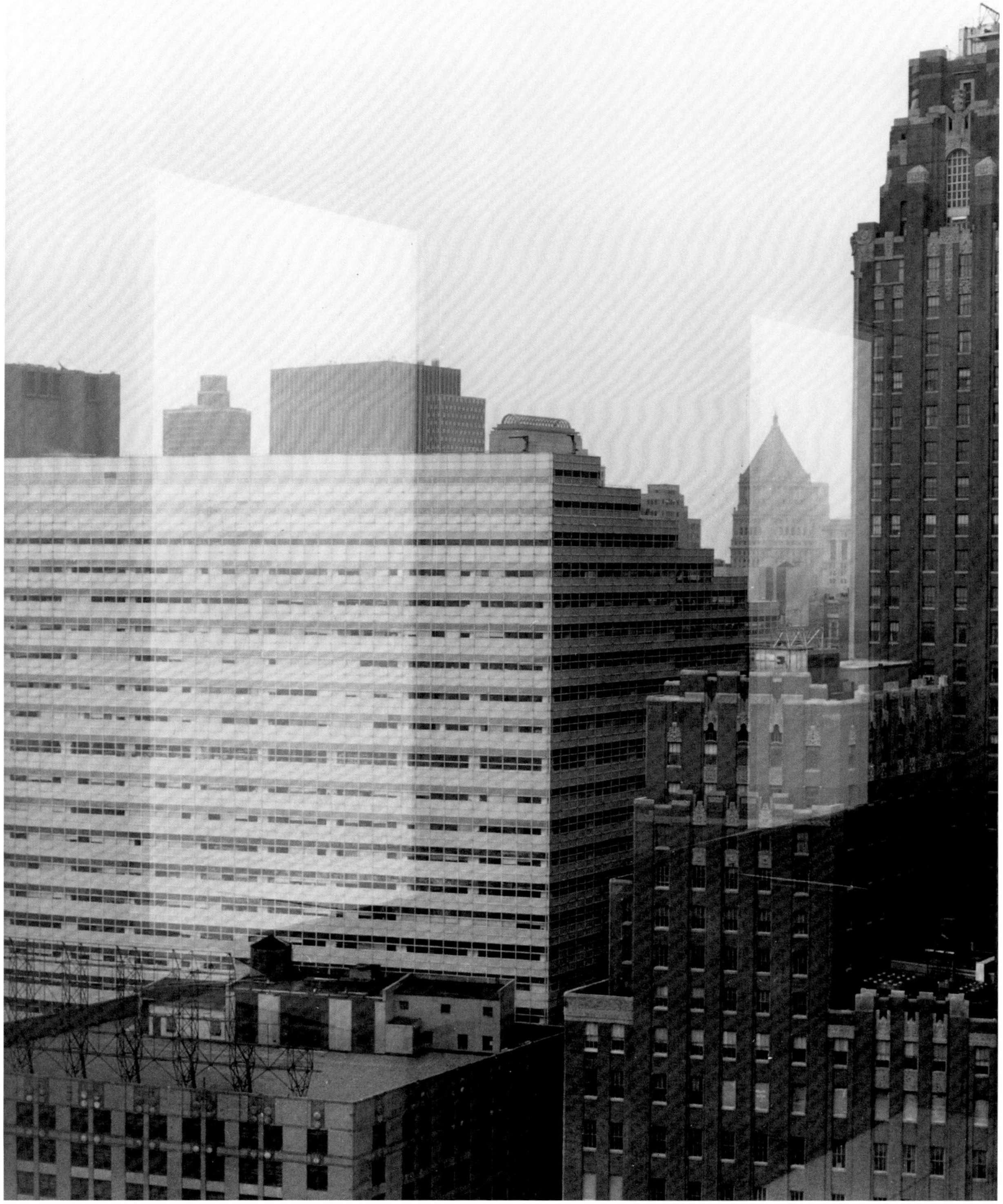

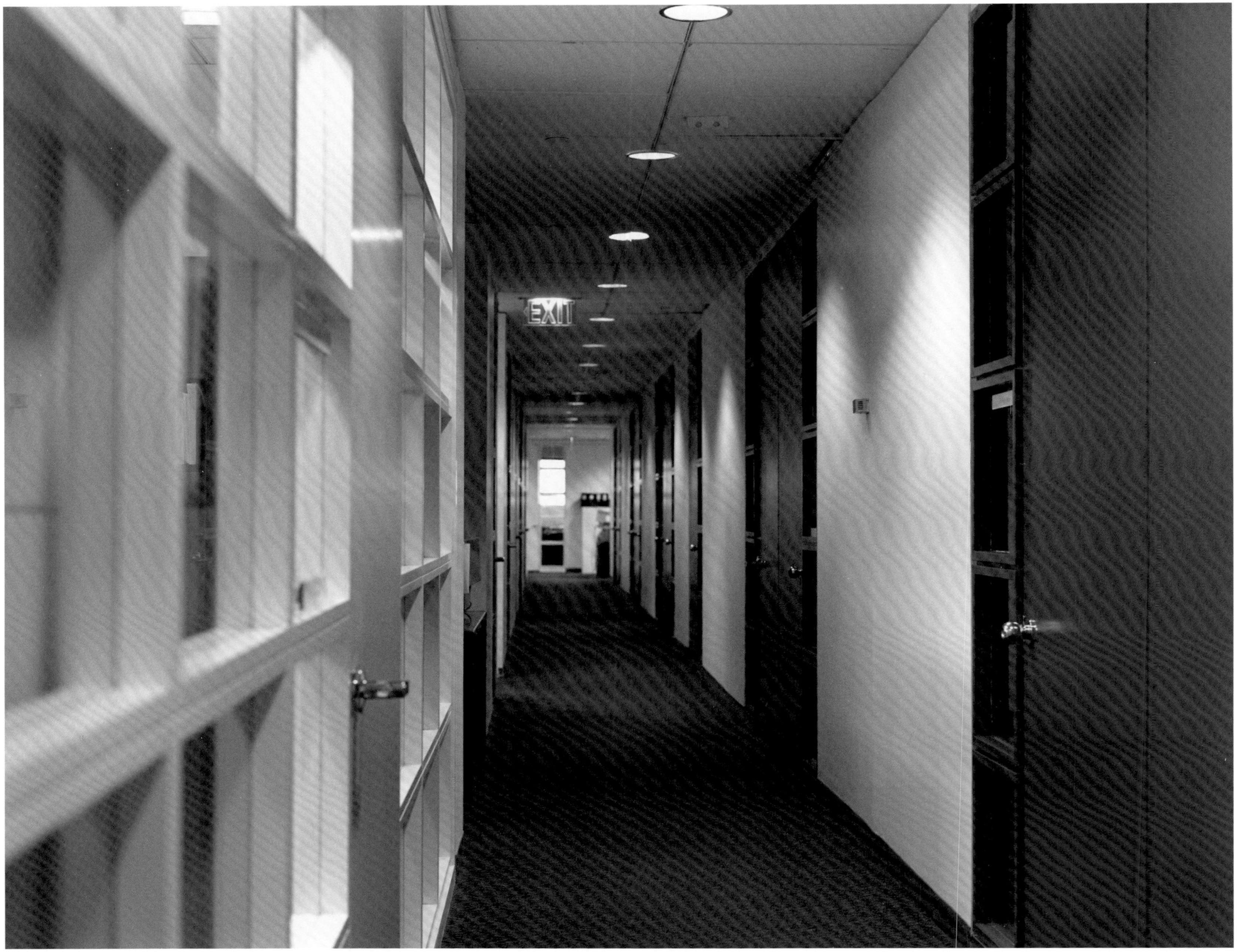
EXIT

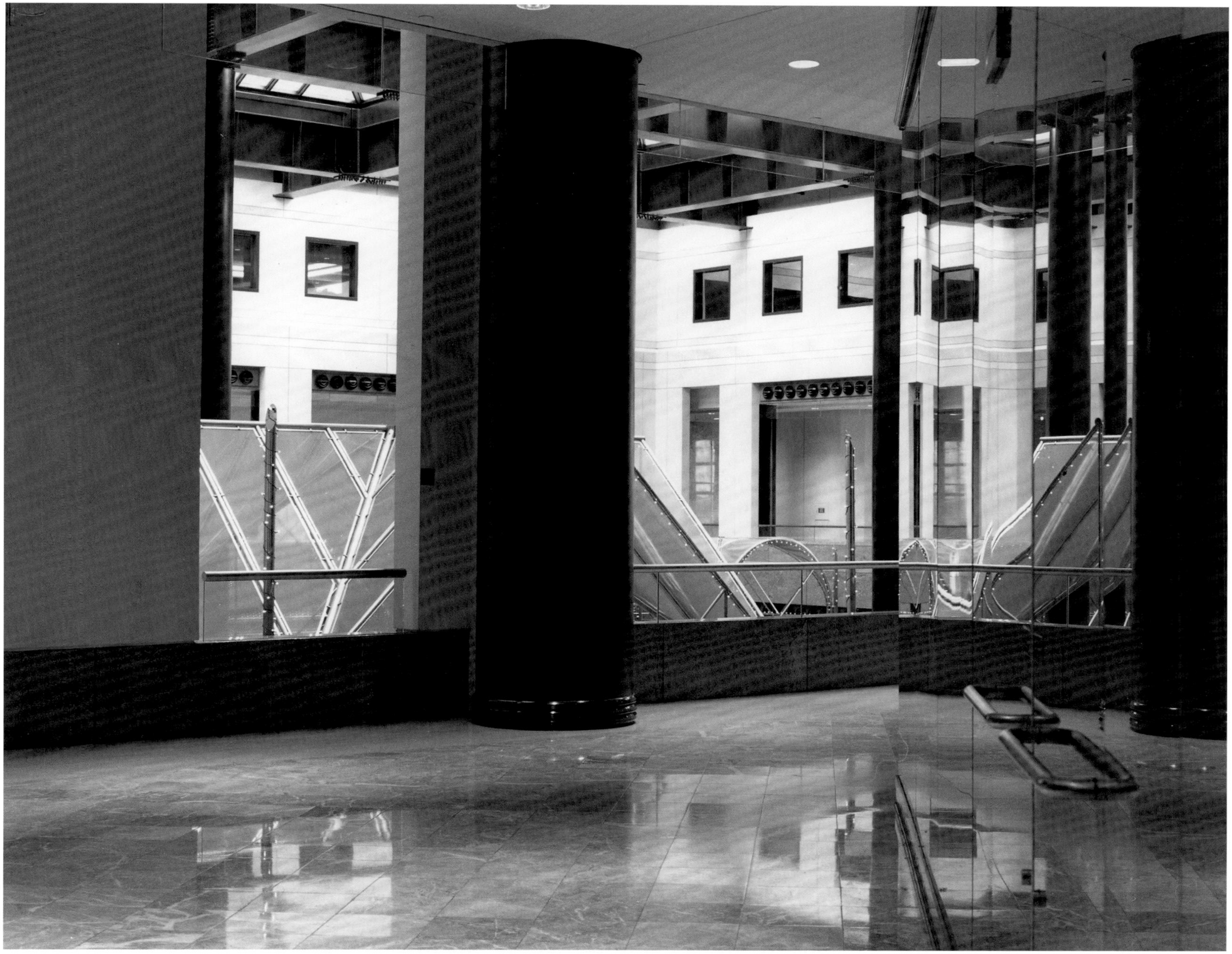

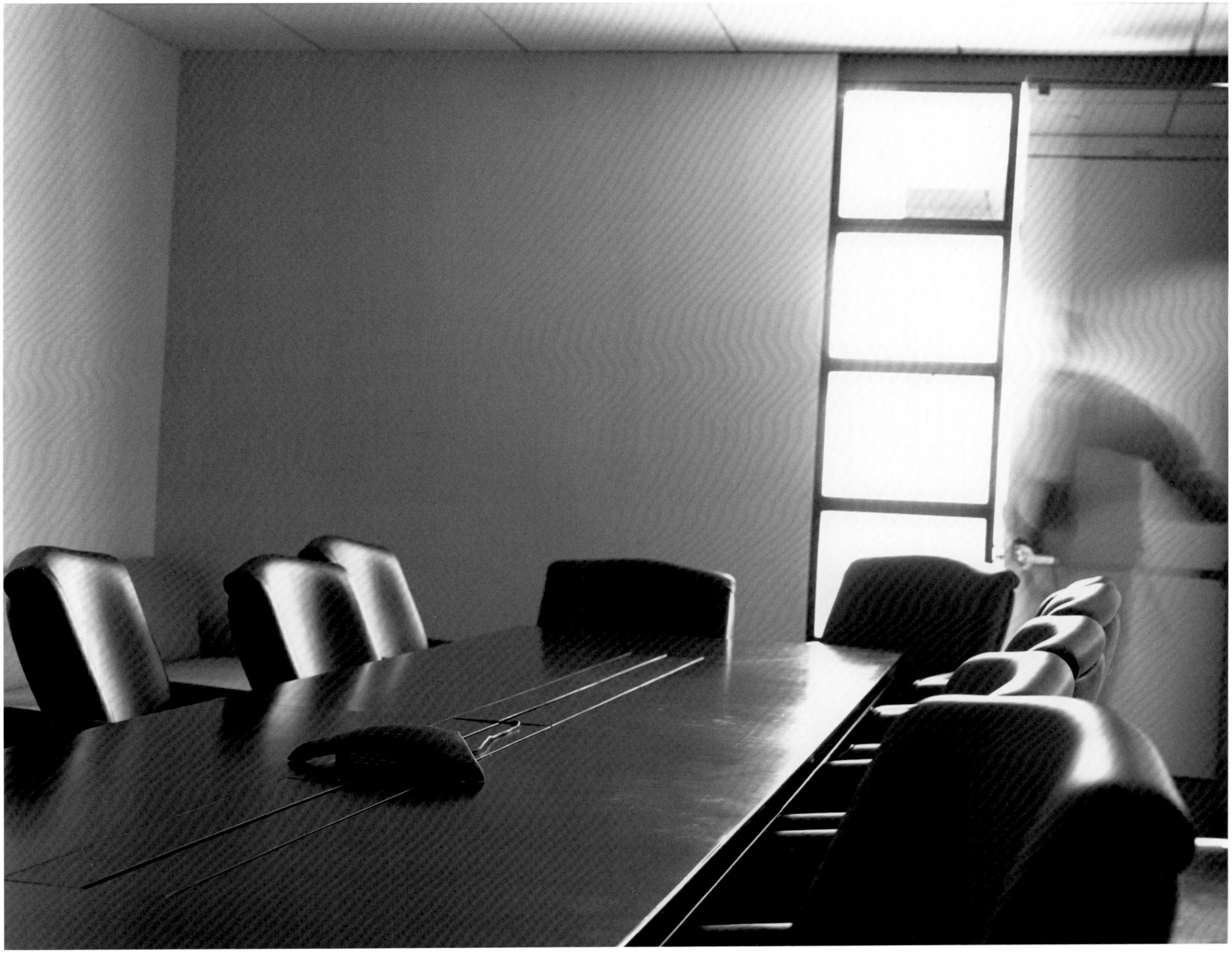

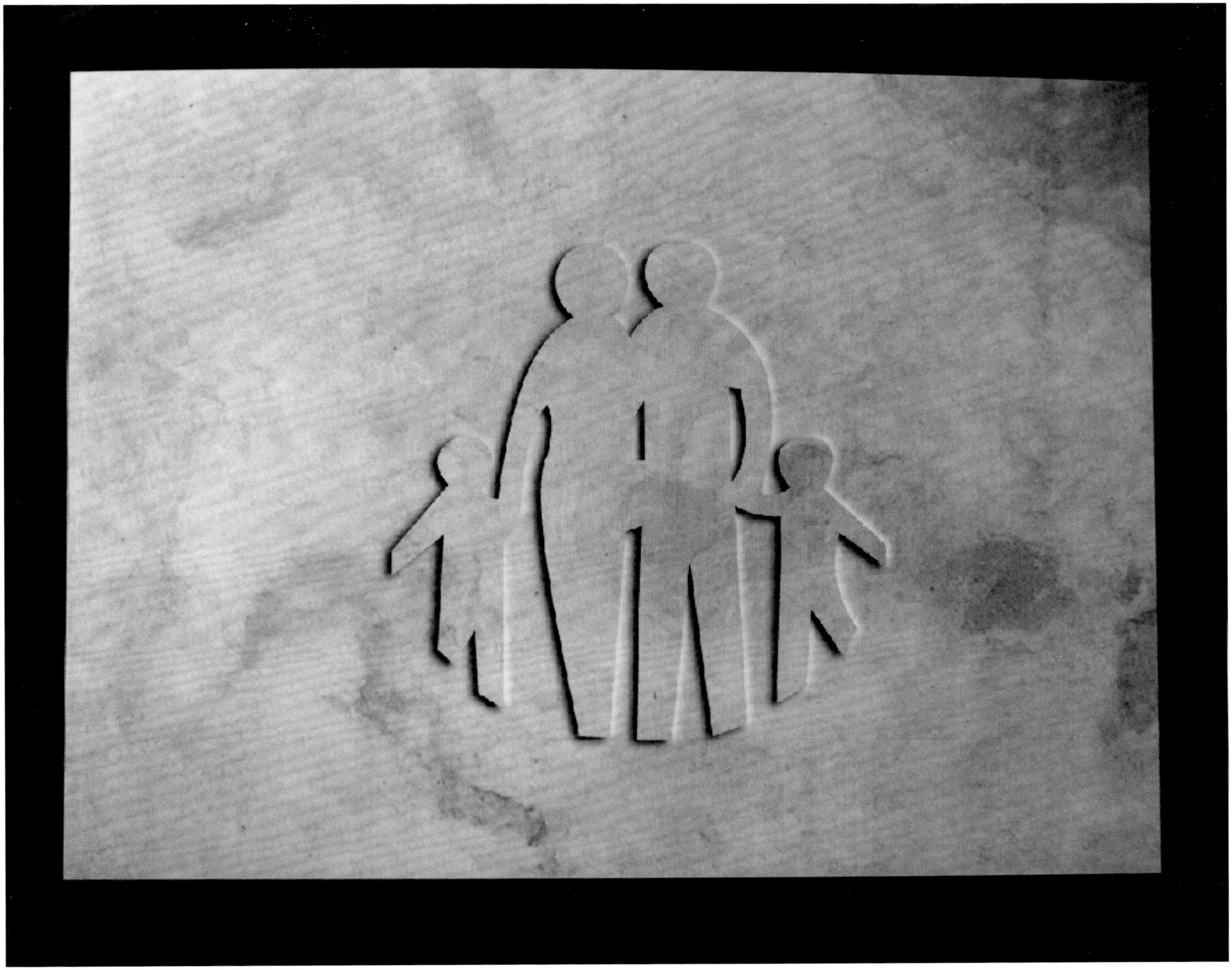

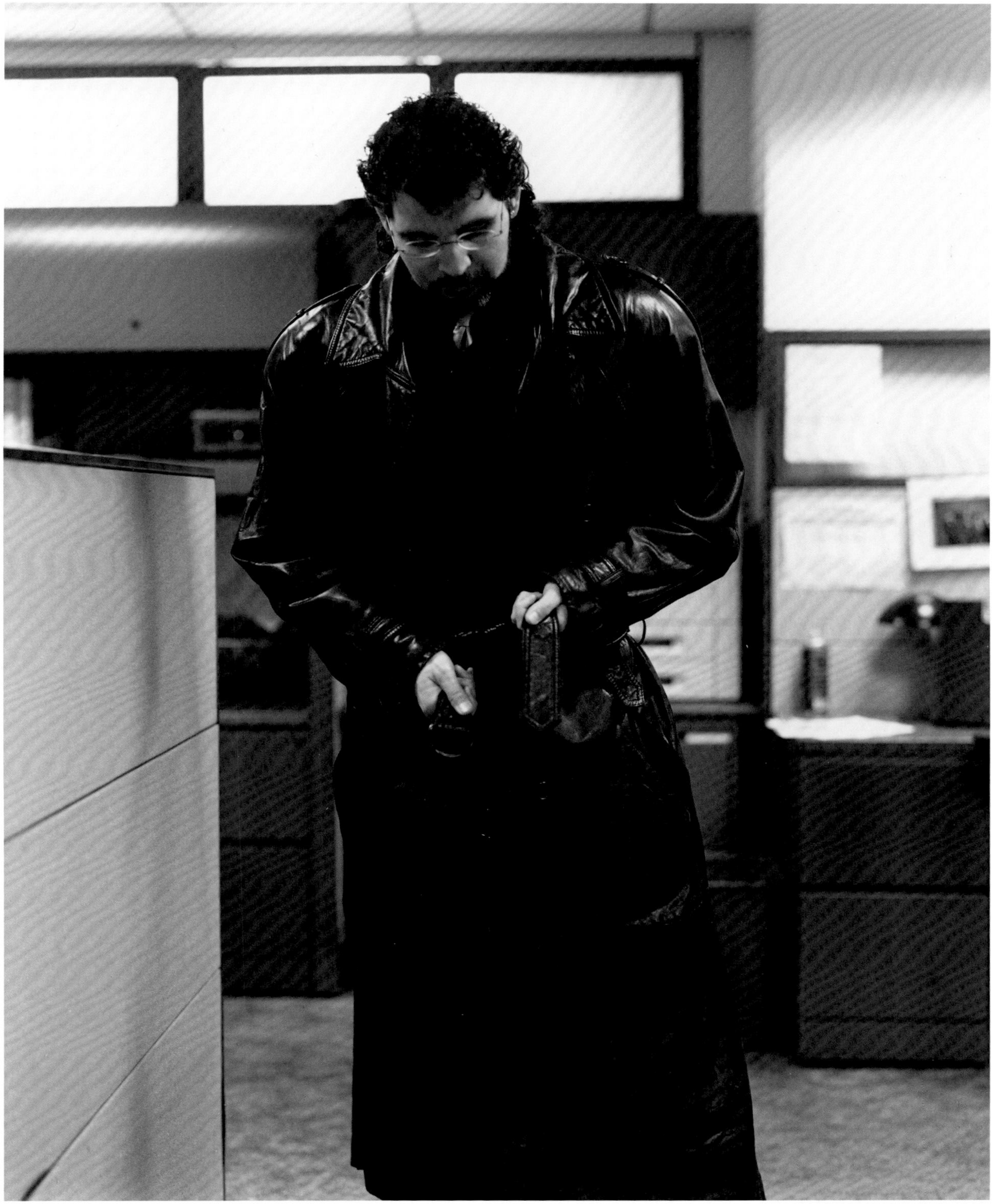

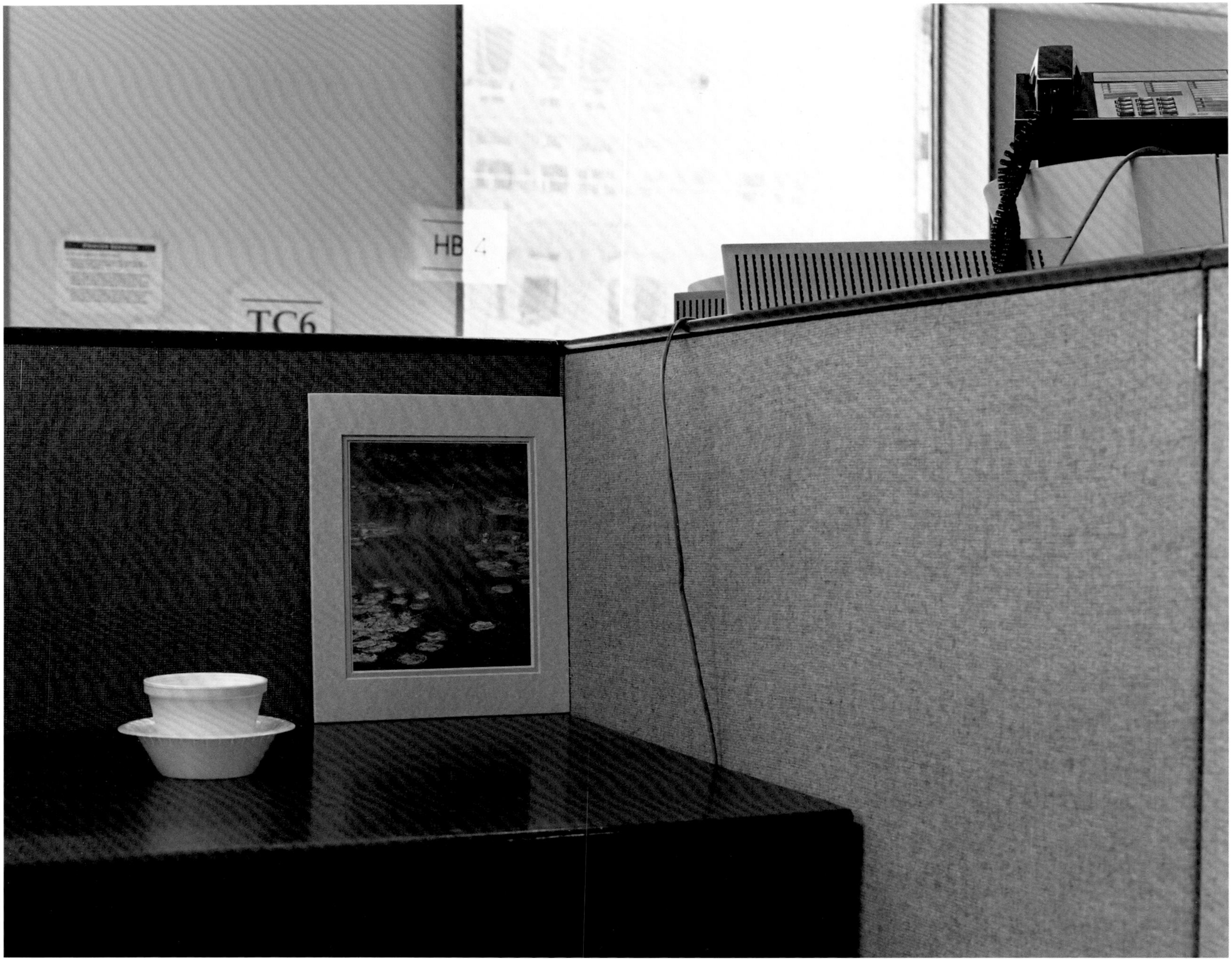
HB 4
TC6

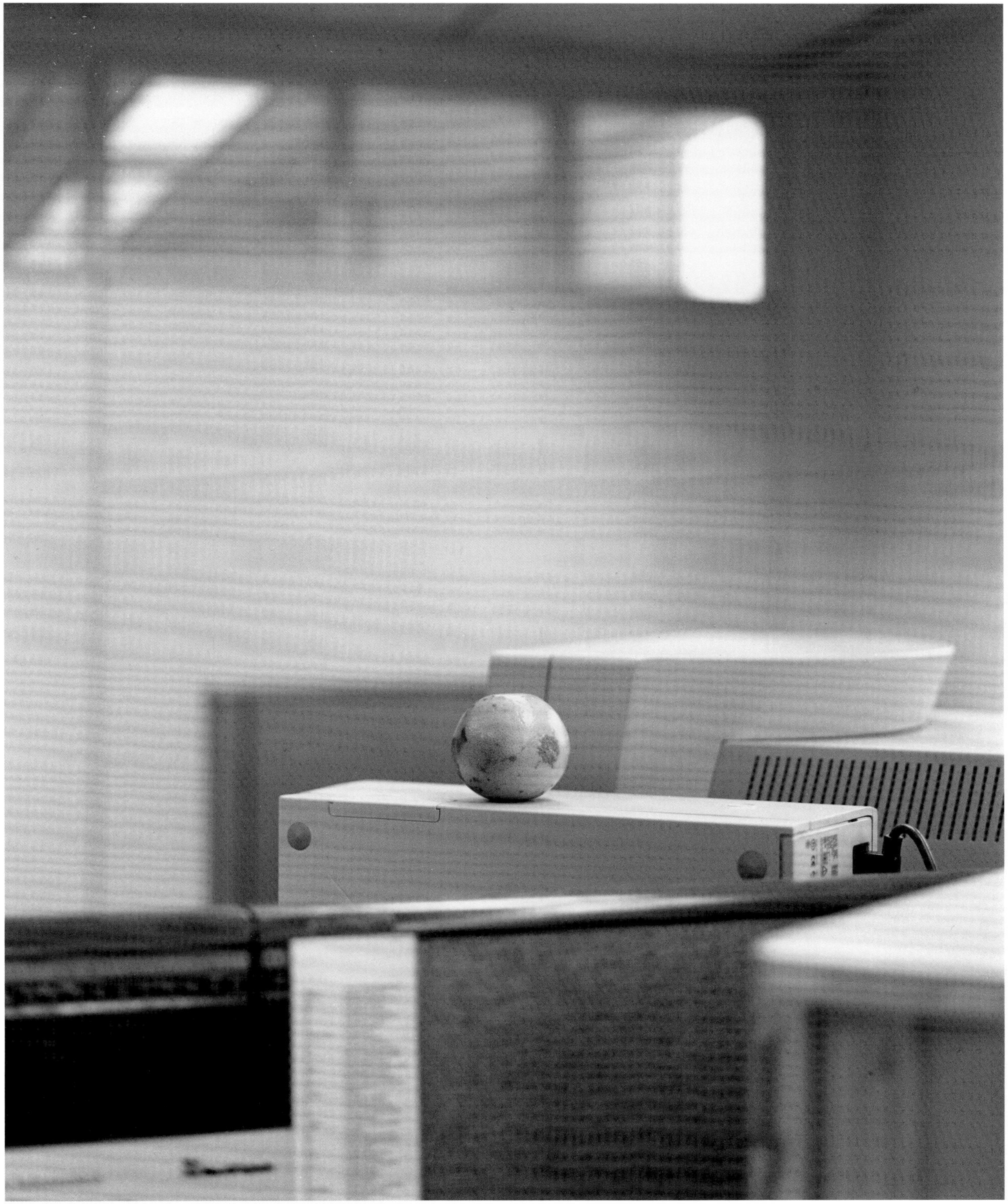

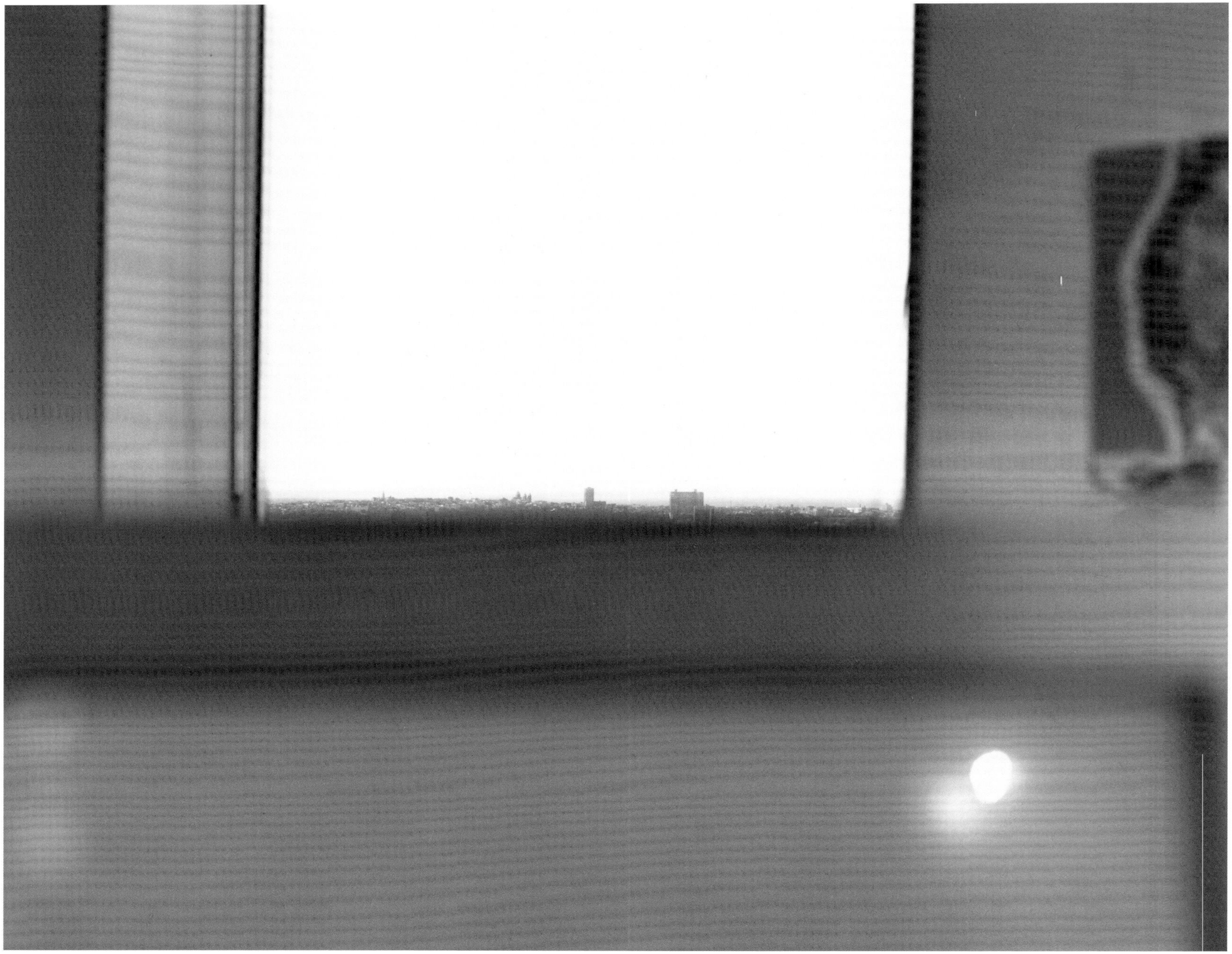

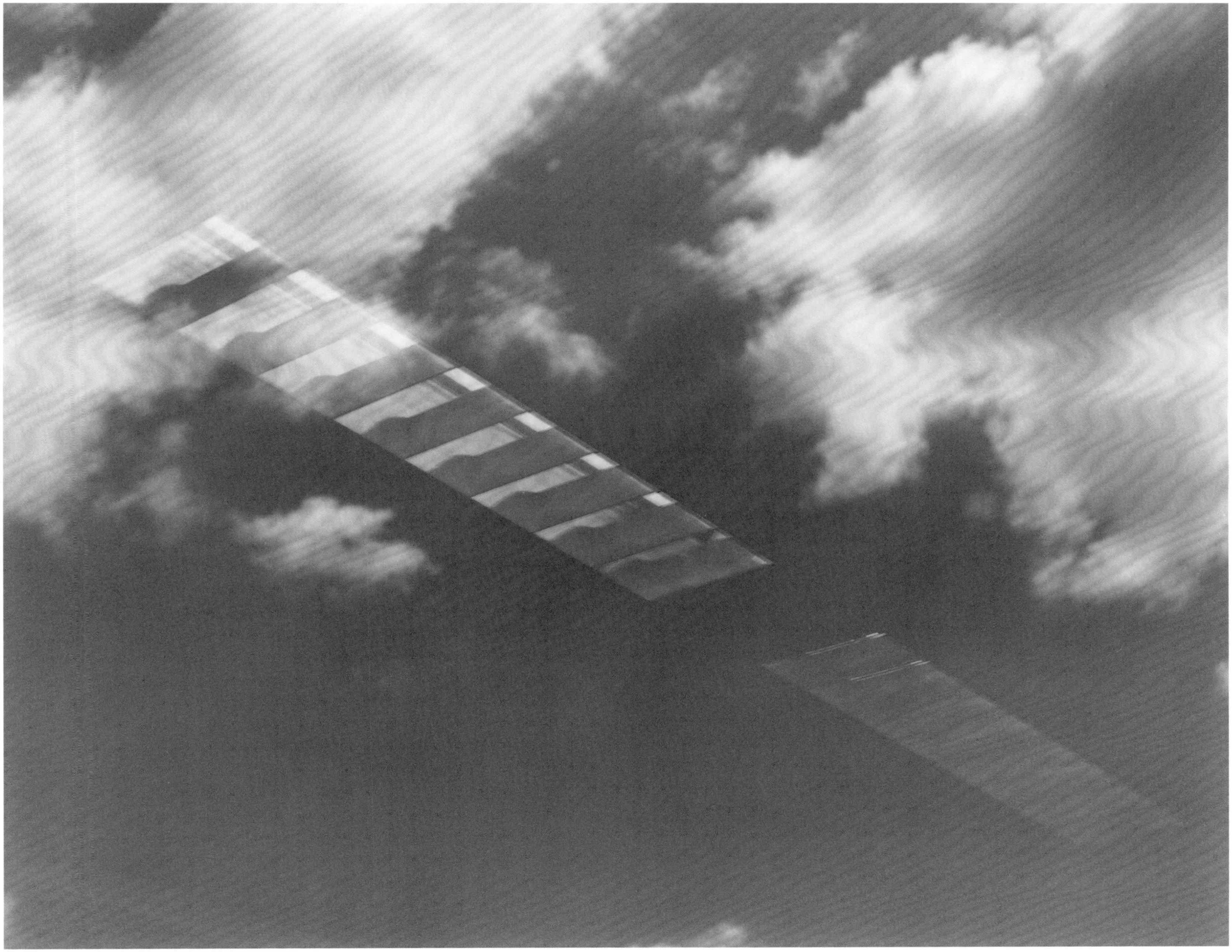

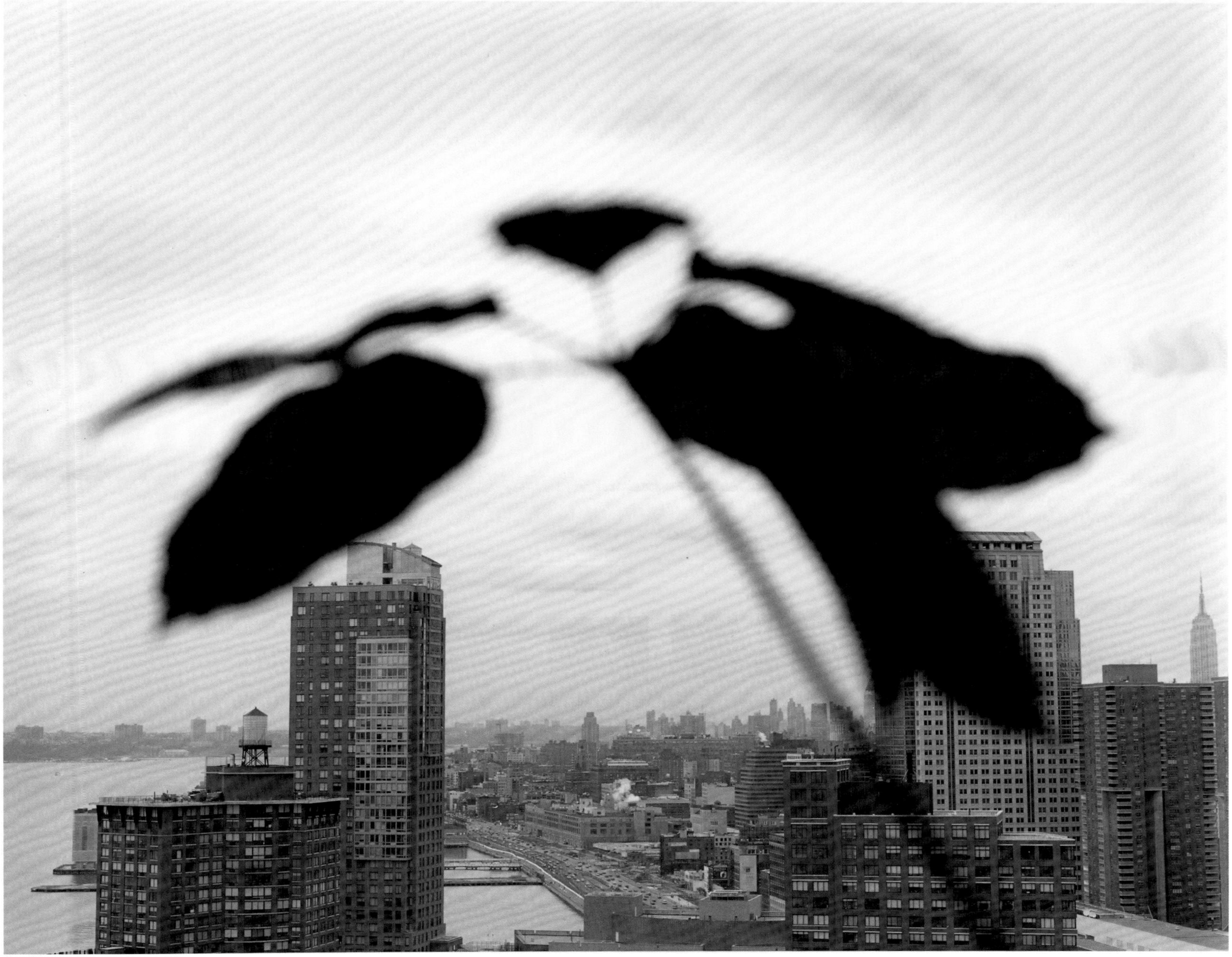

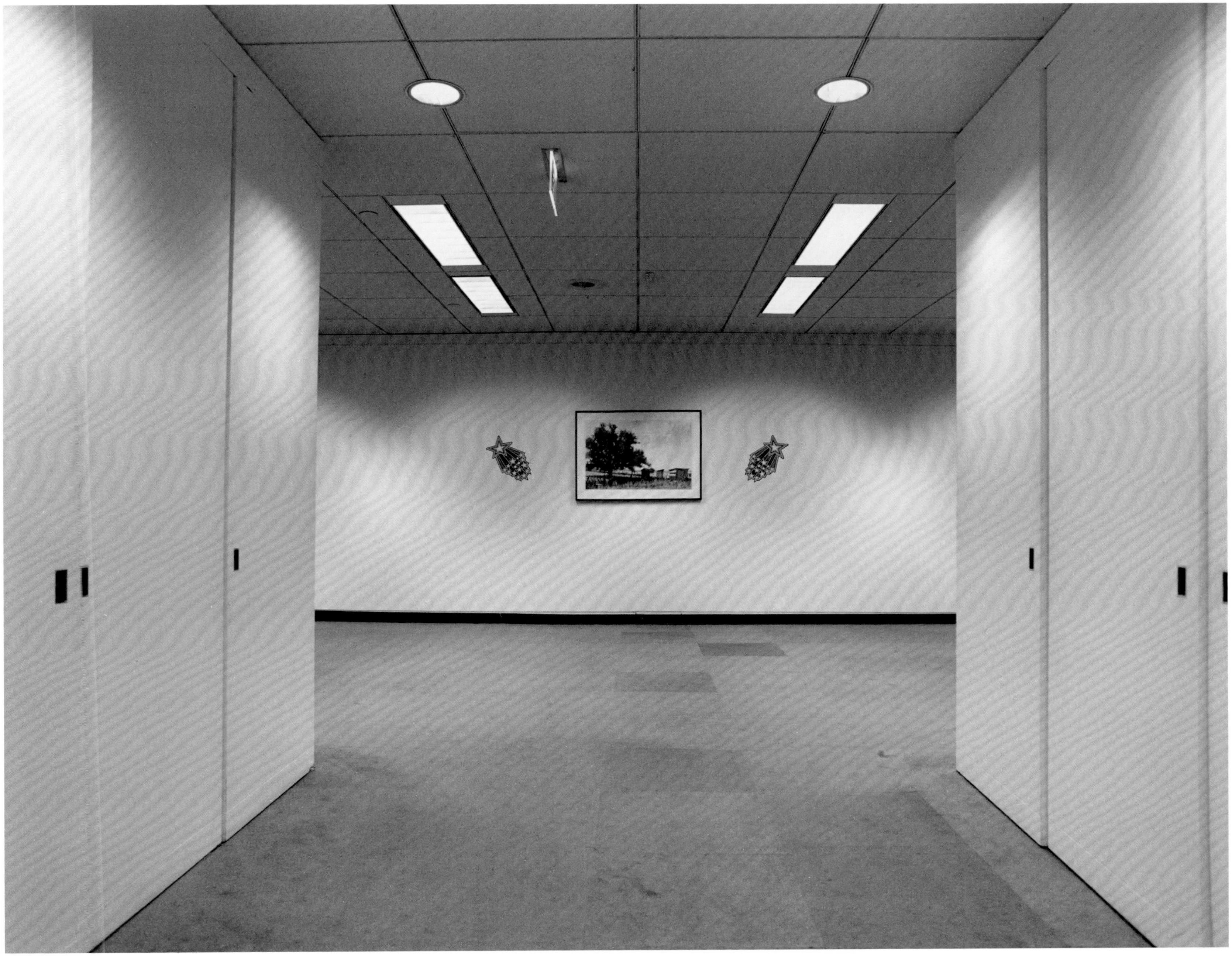

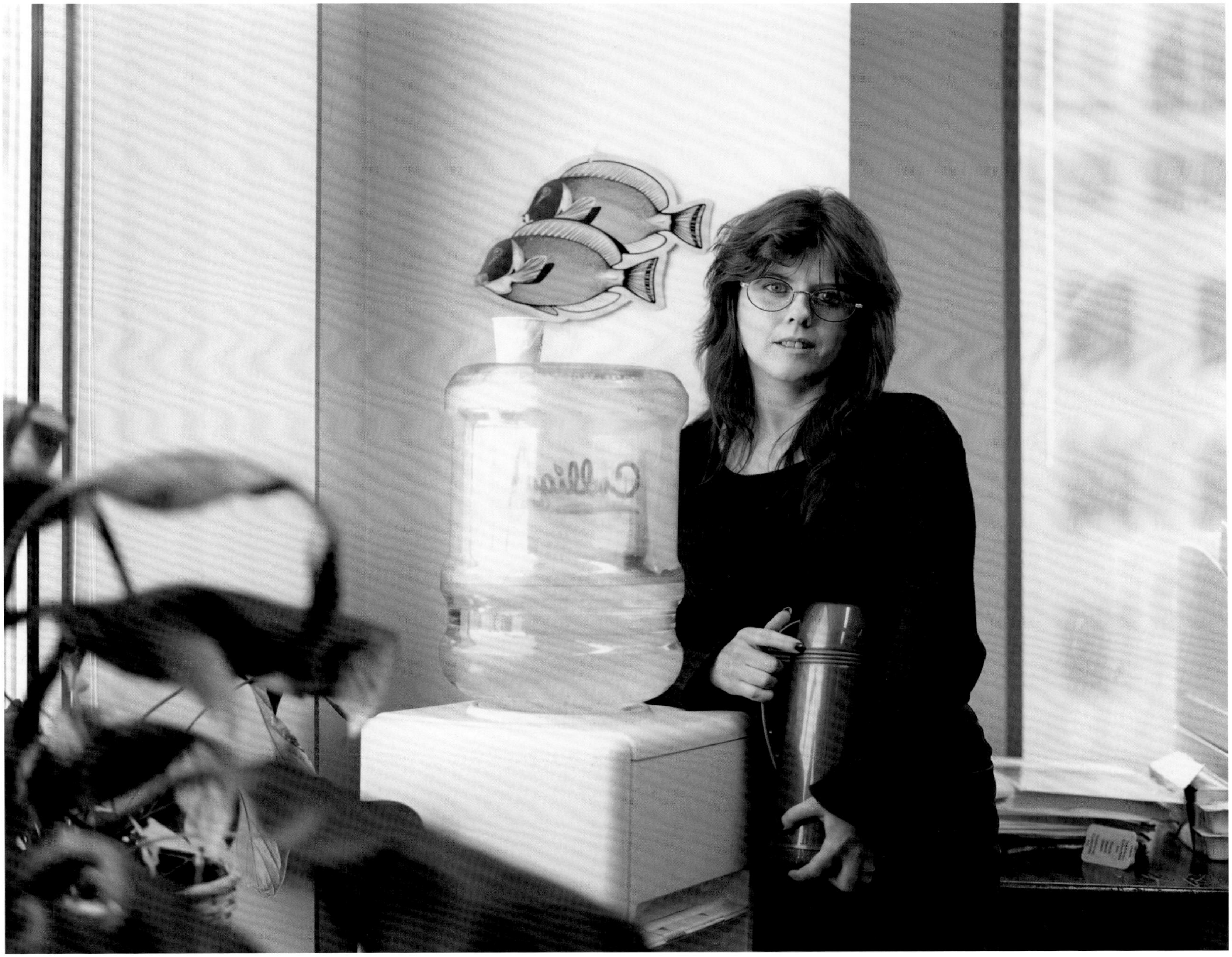

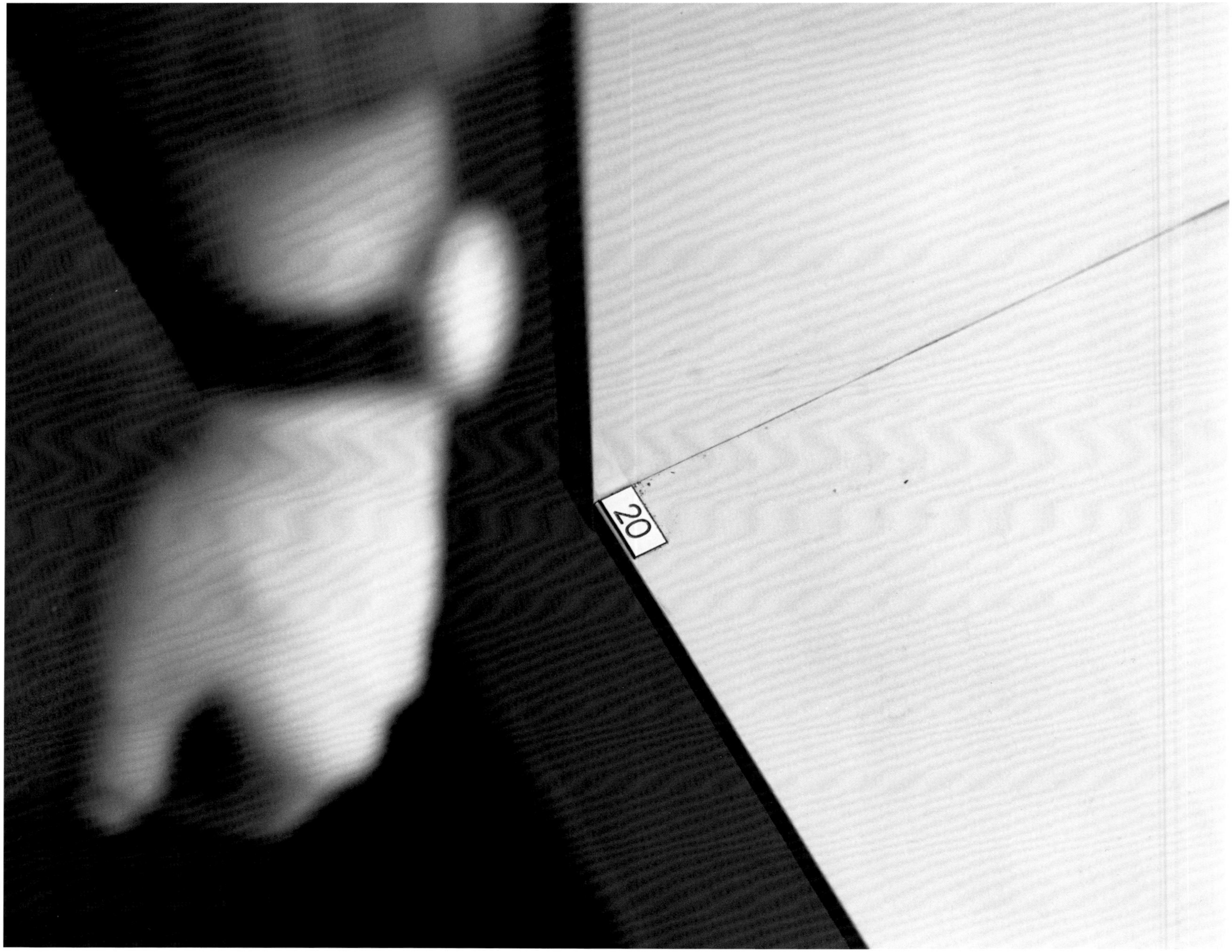
20

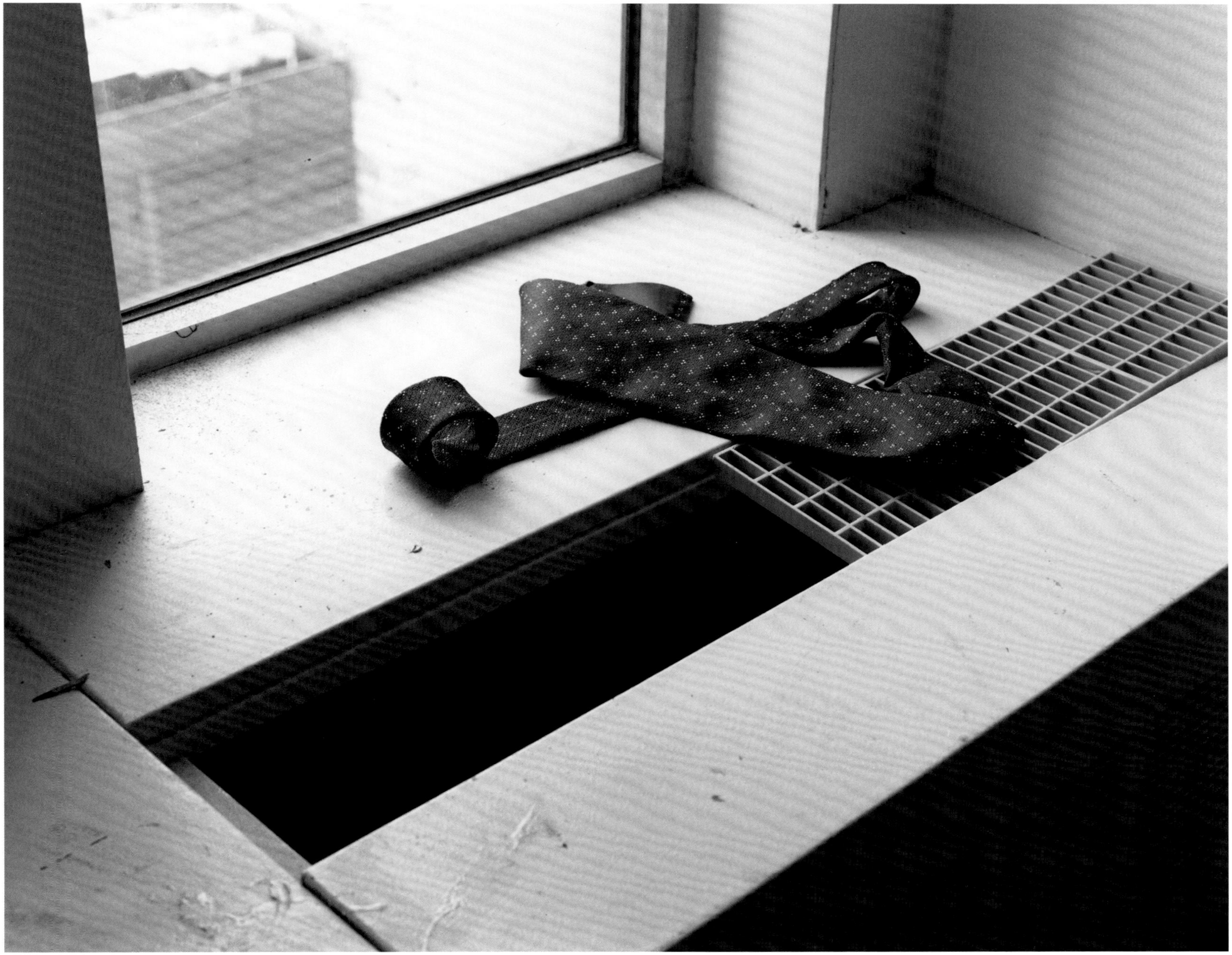

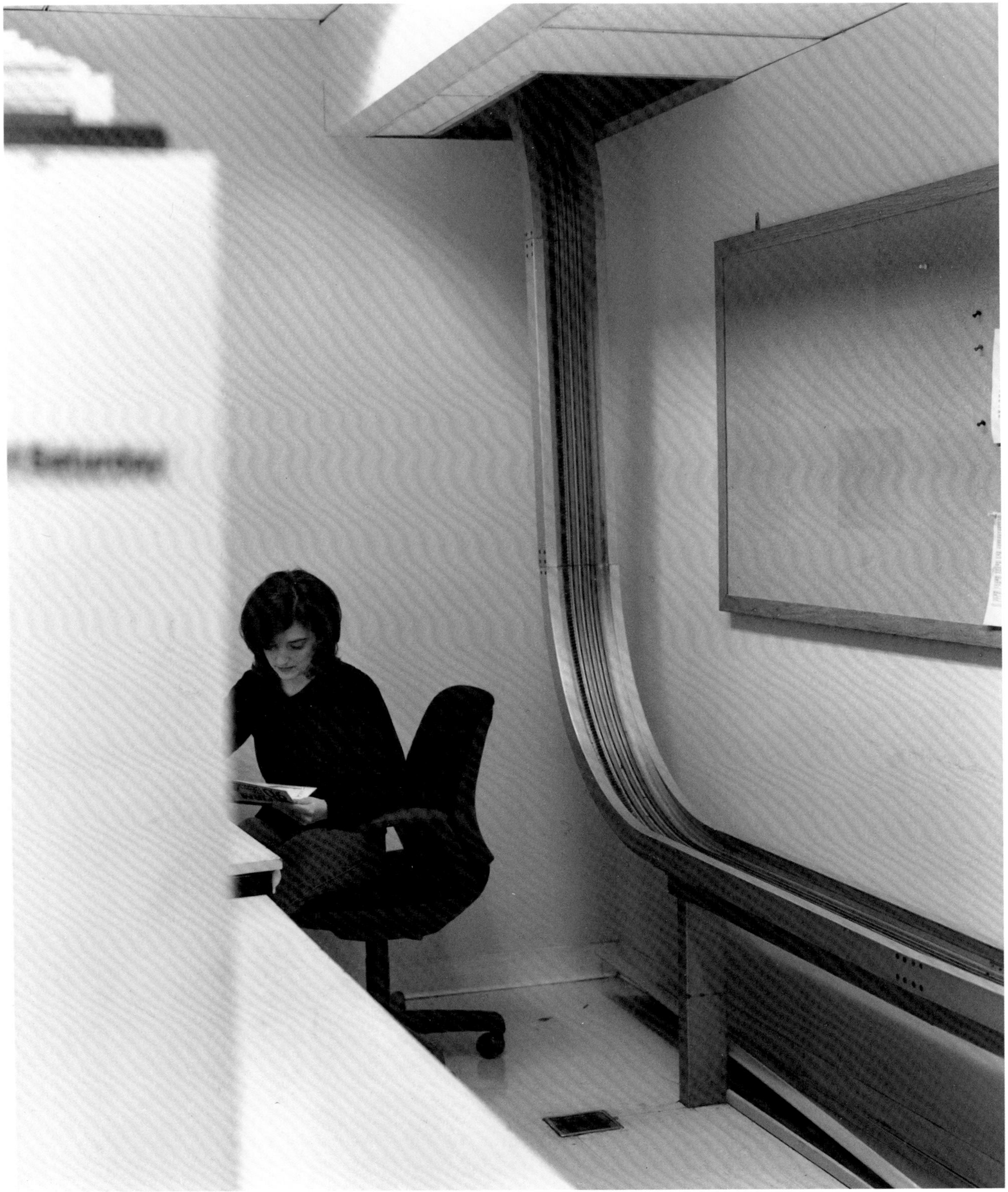

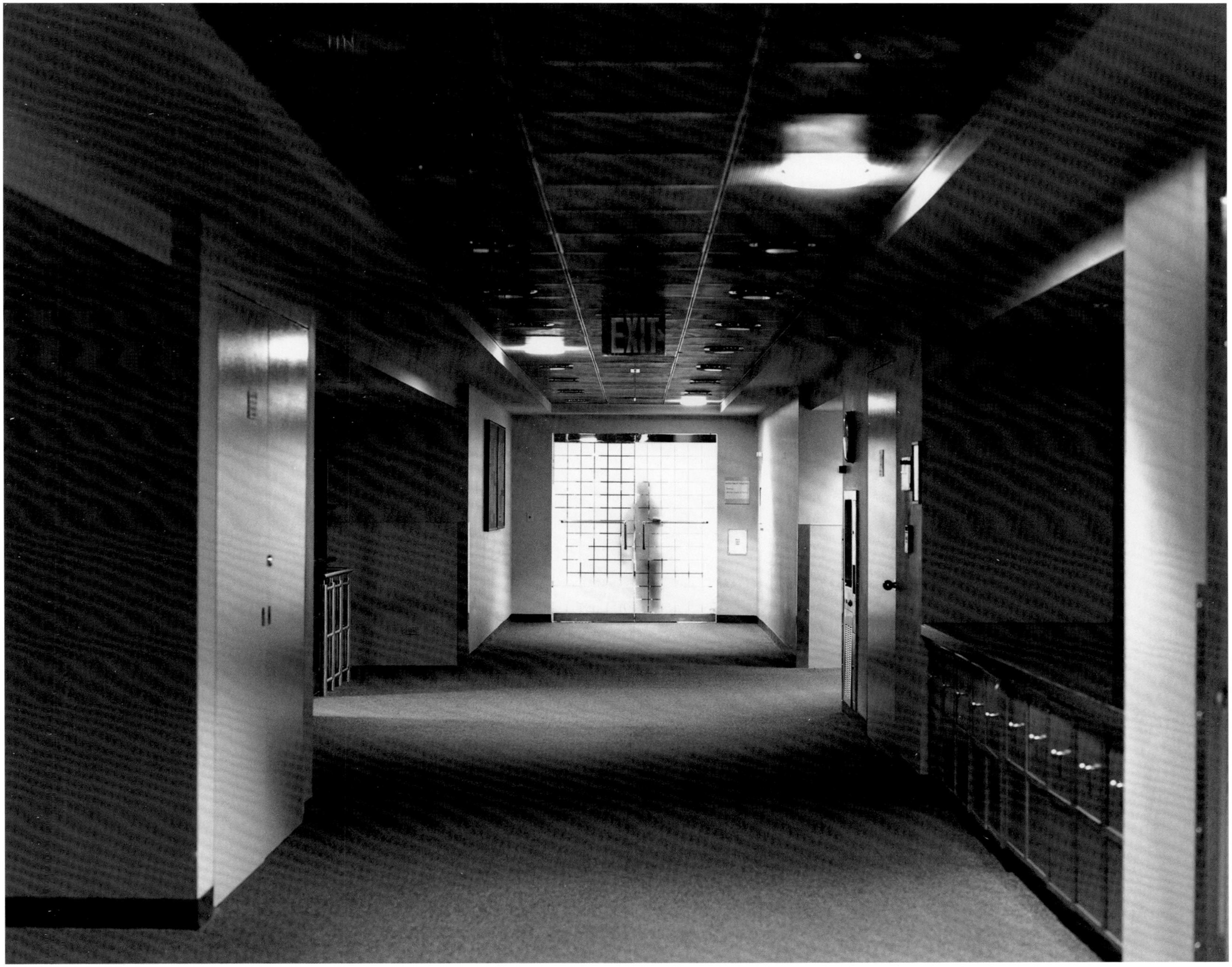
EXIT

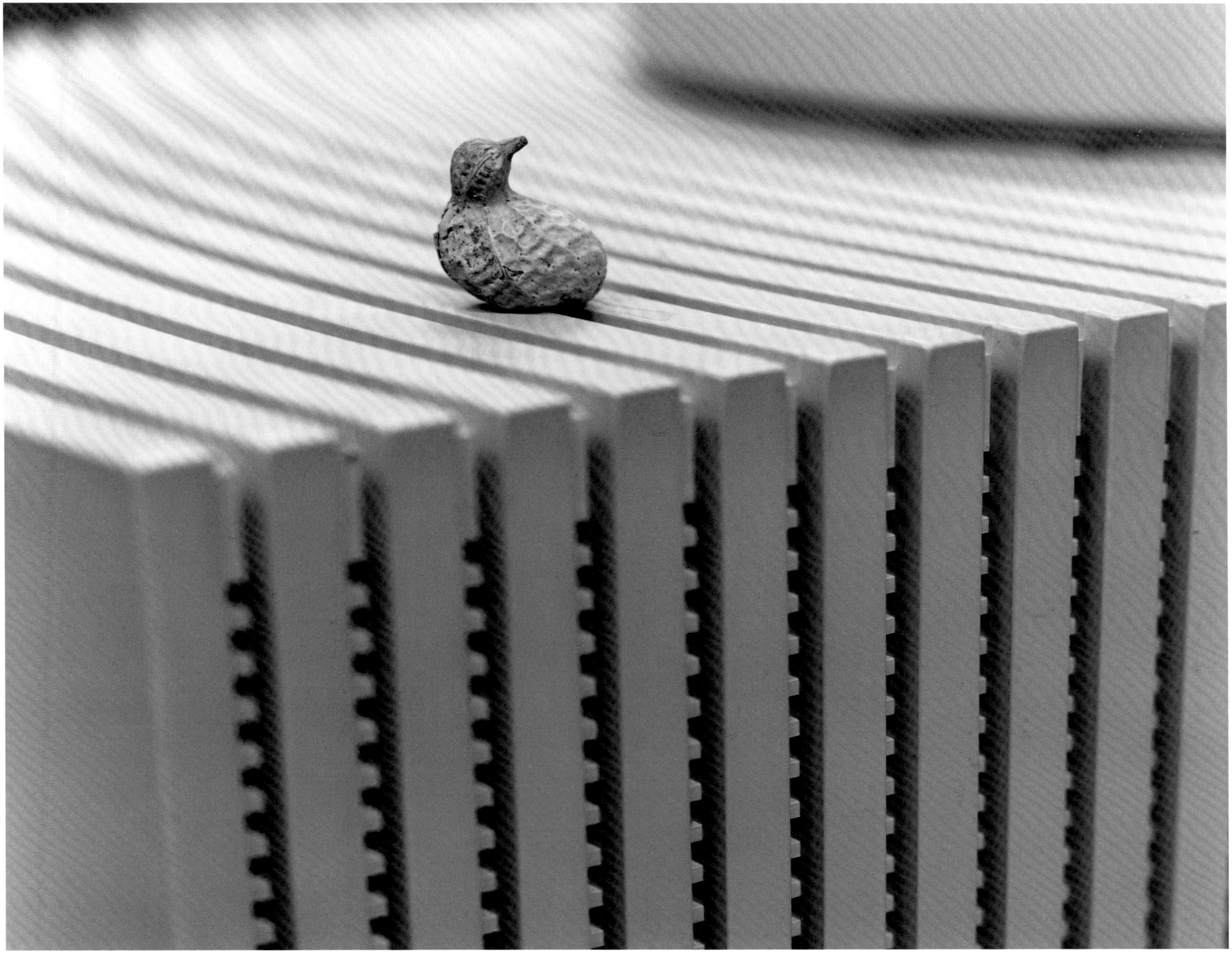

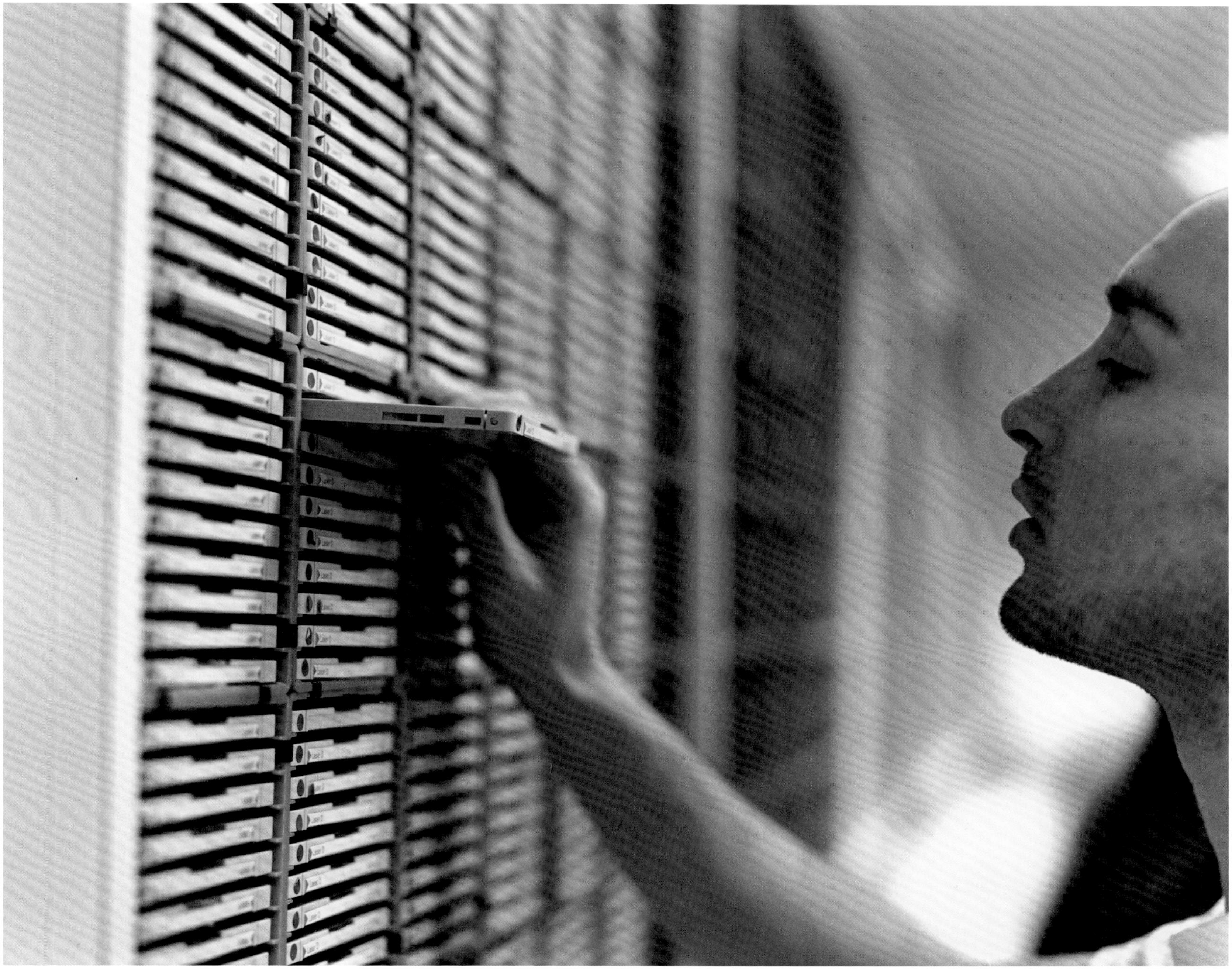

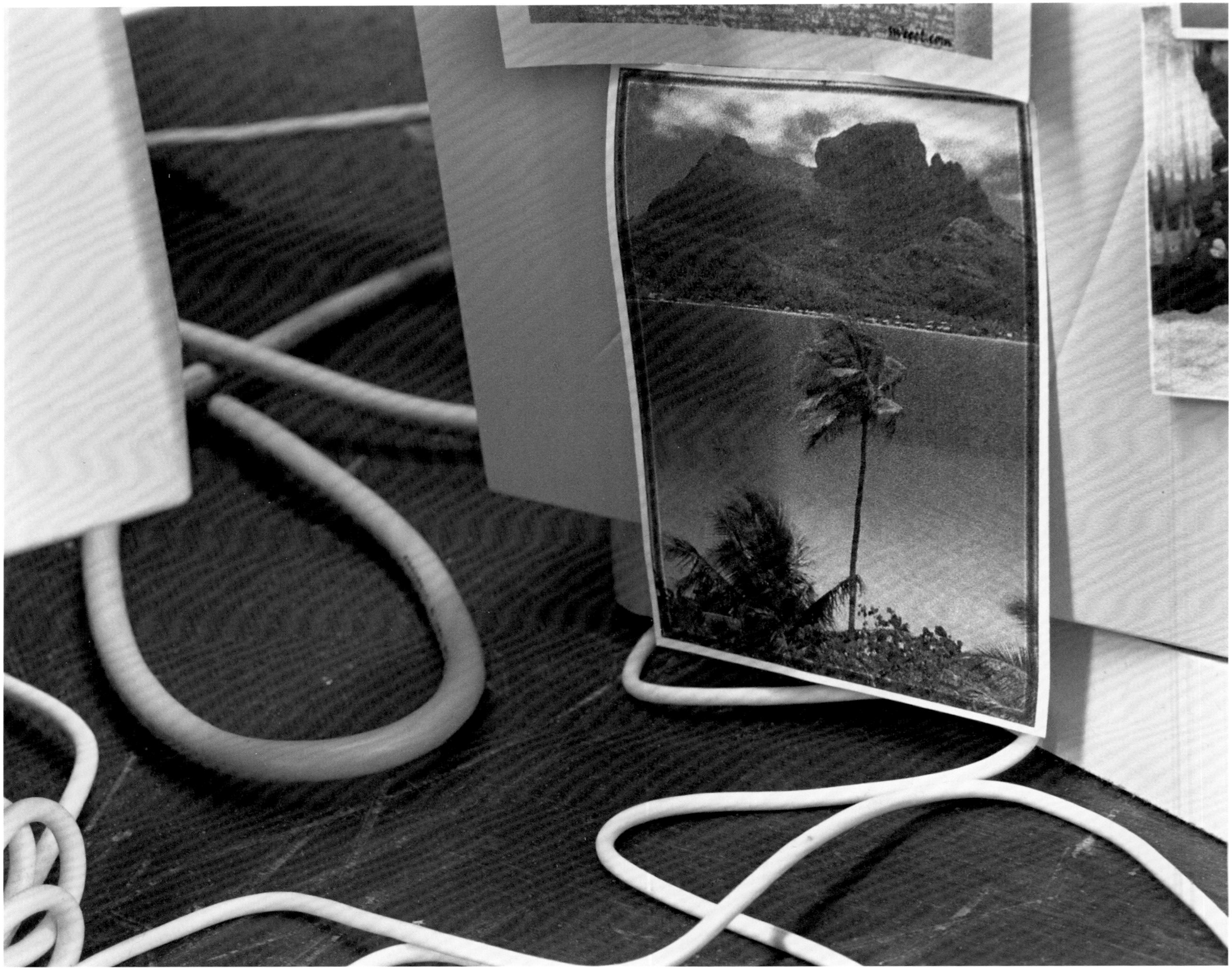

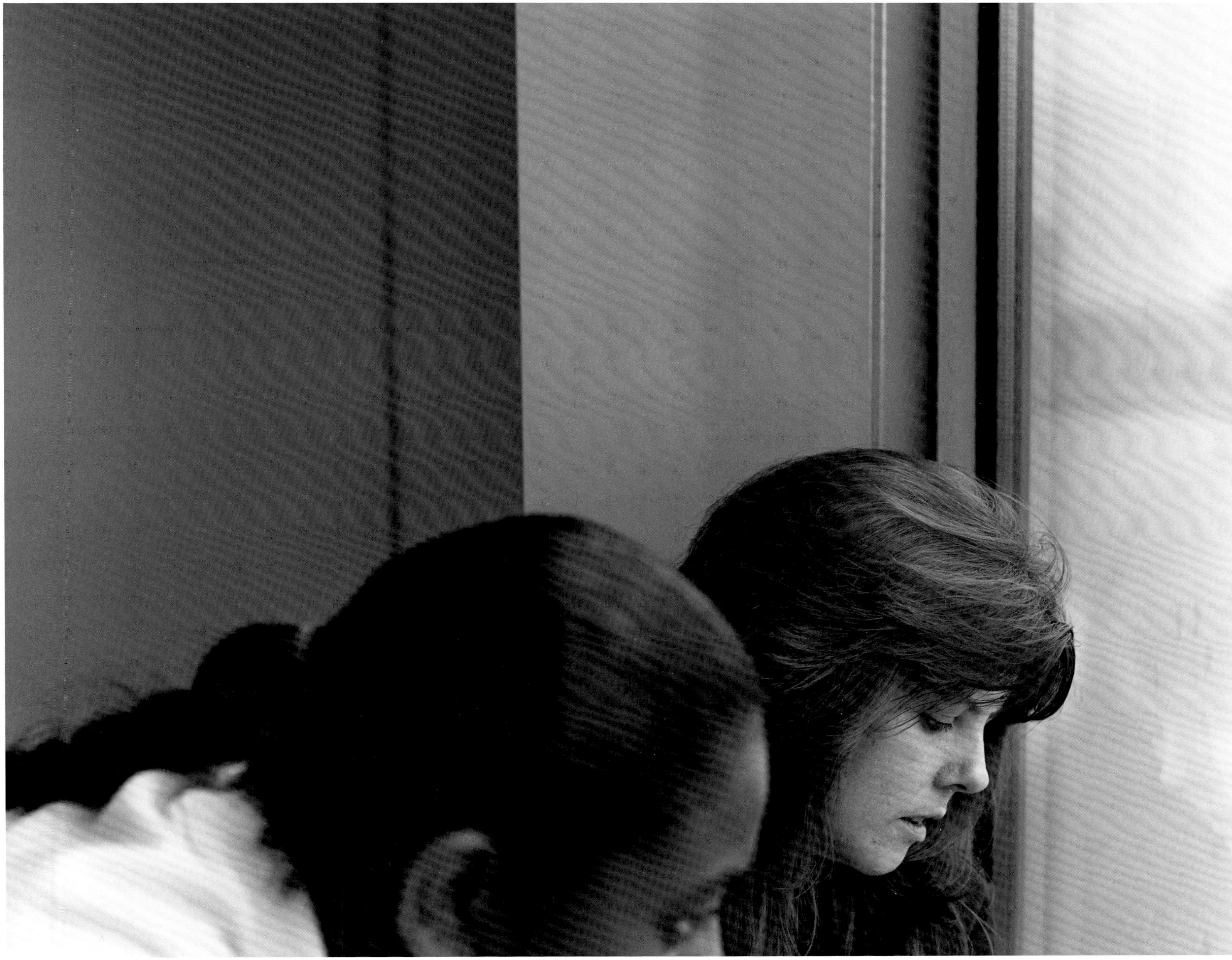

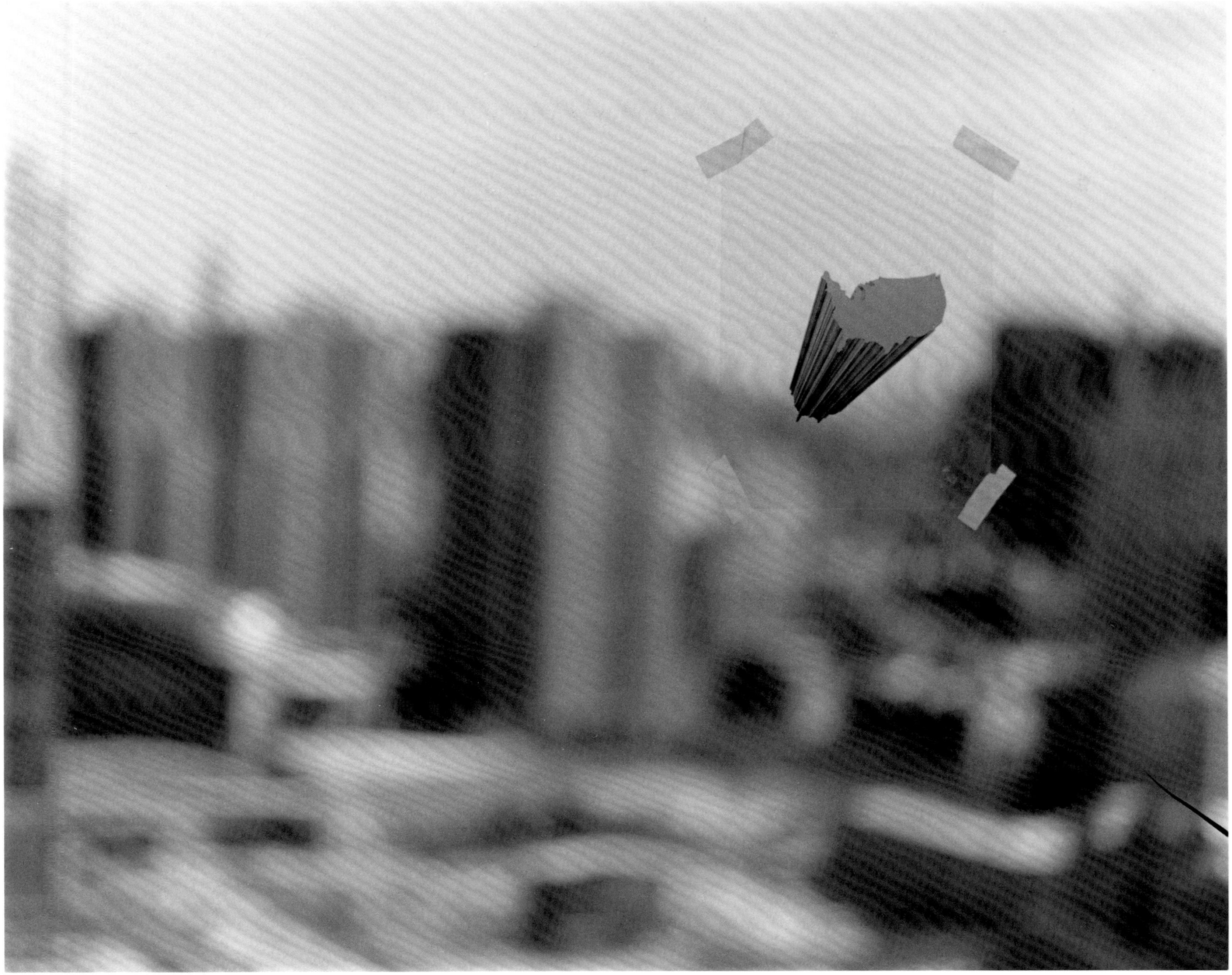

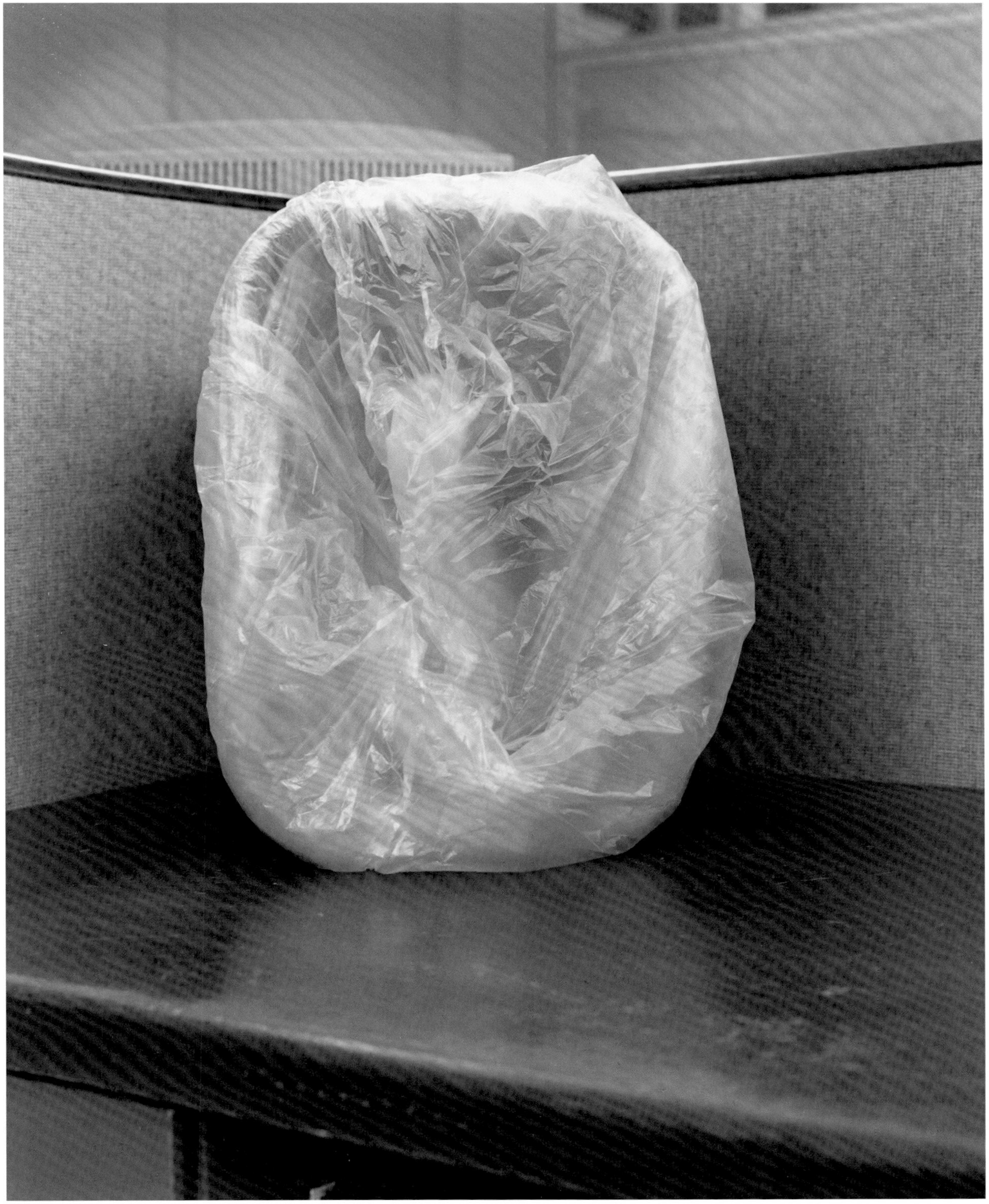

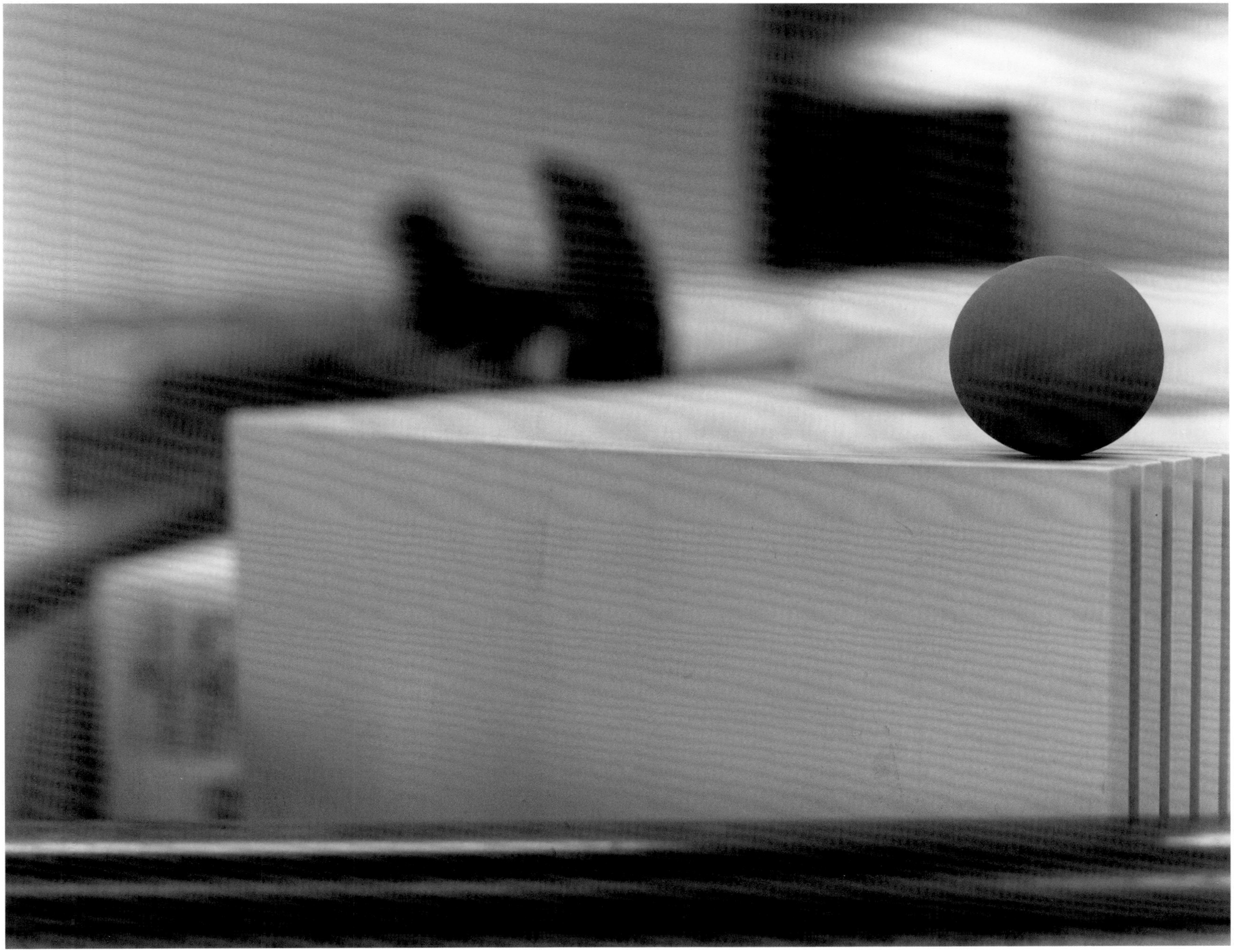

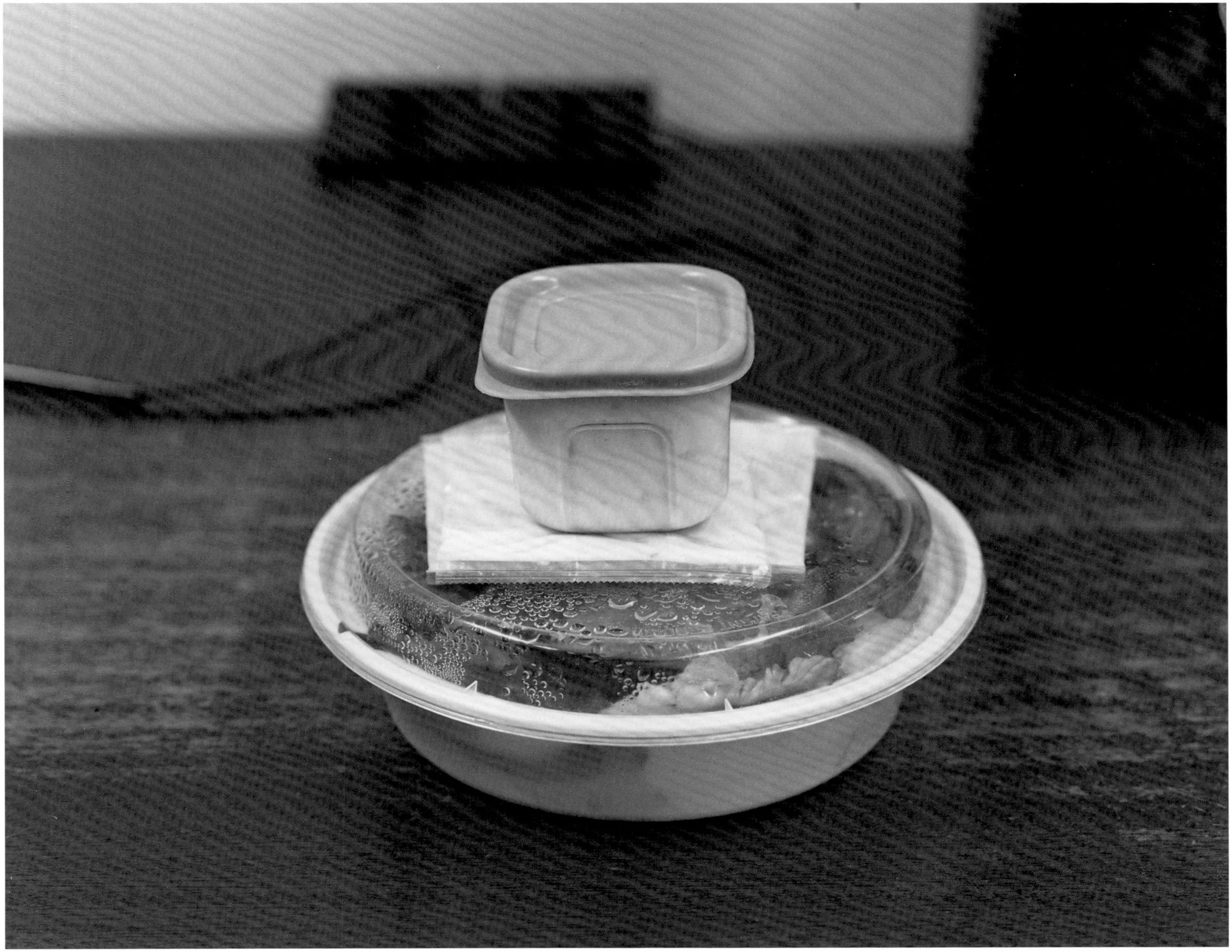

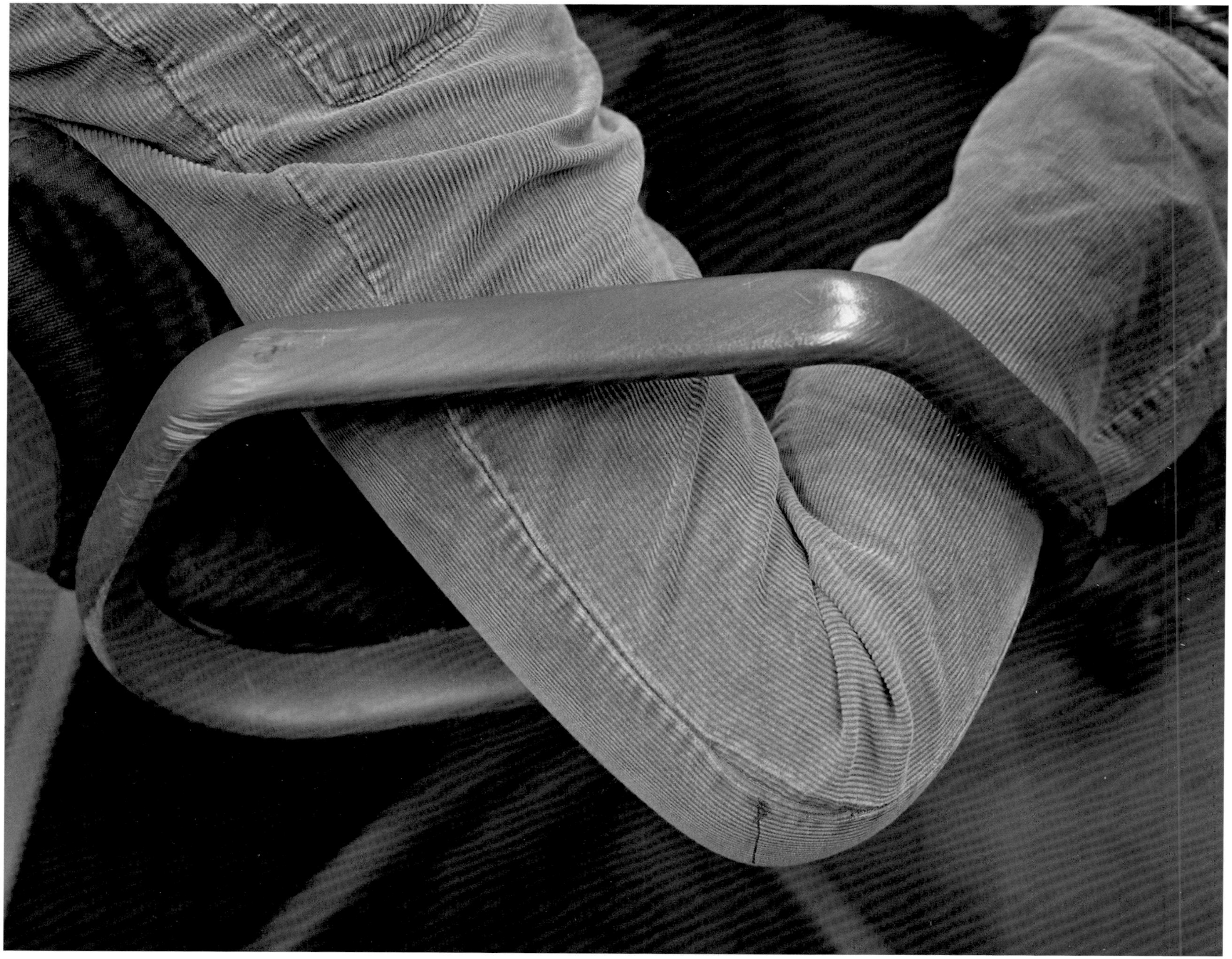

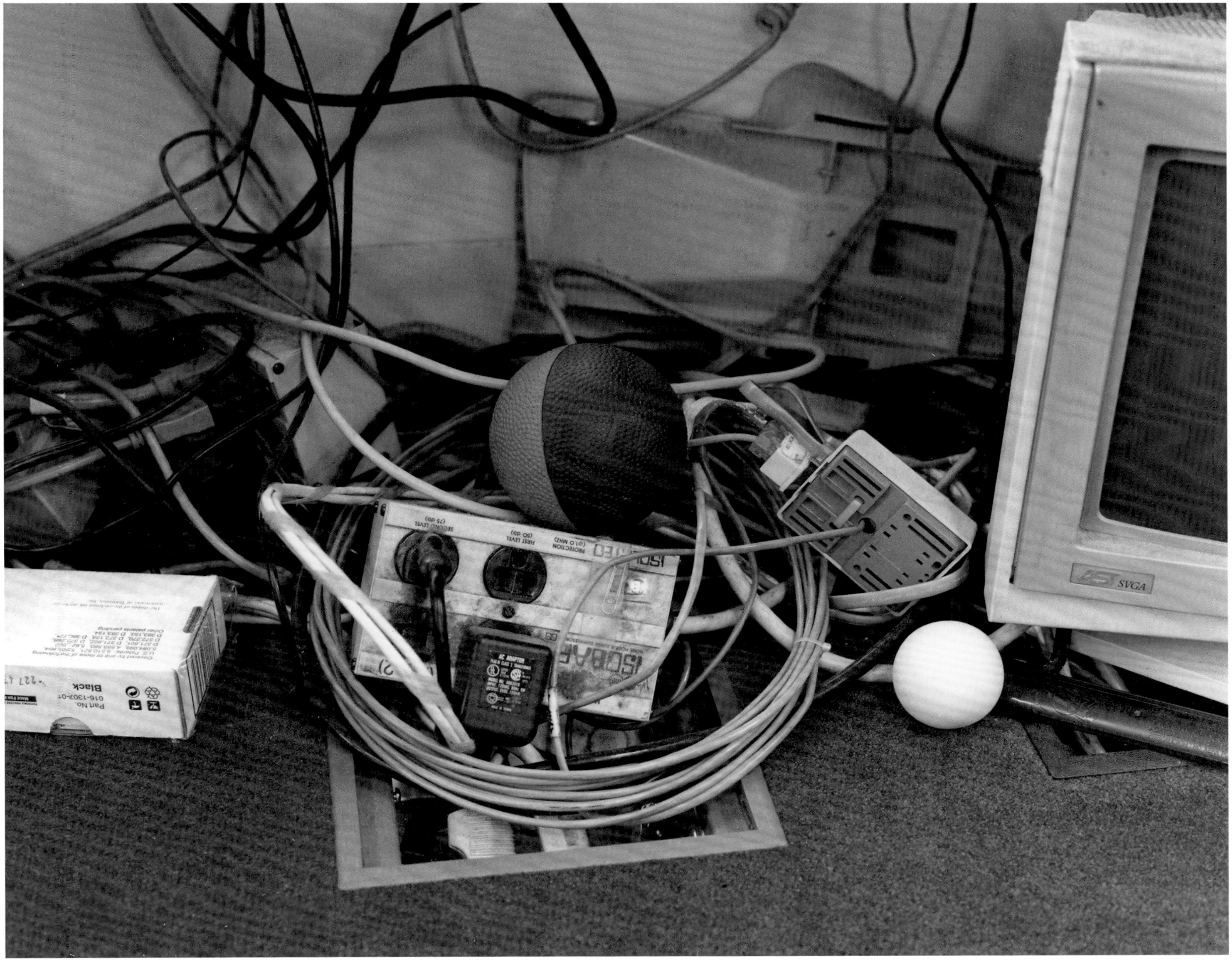
AC ADAPTOR
SVGA

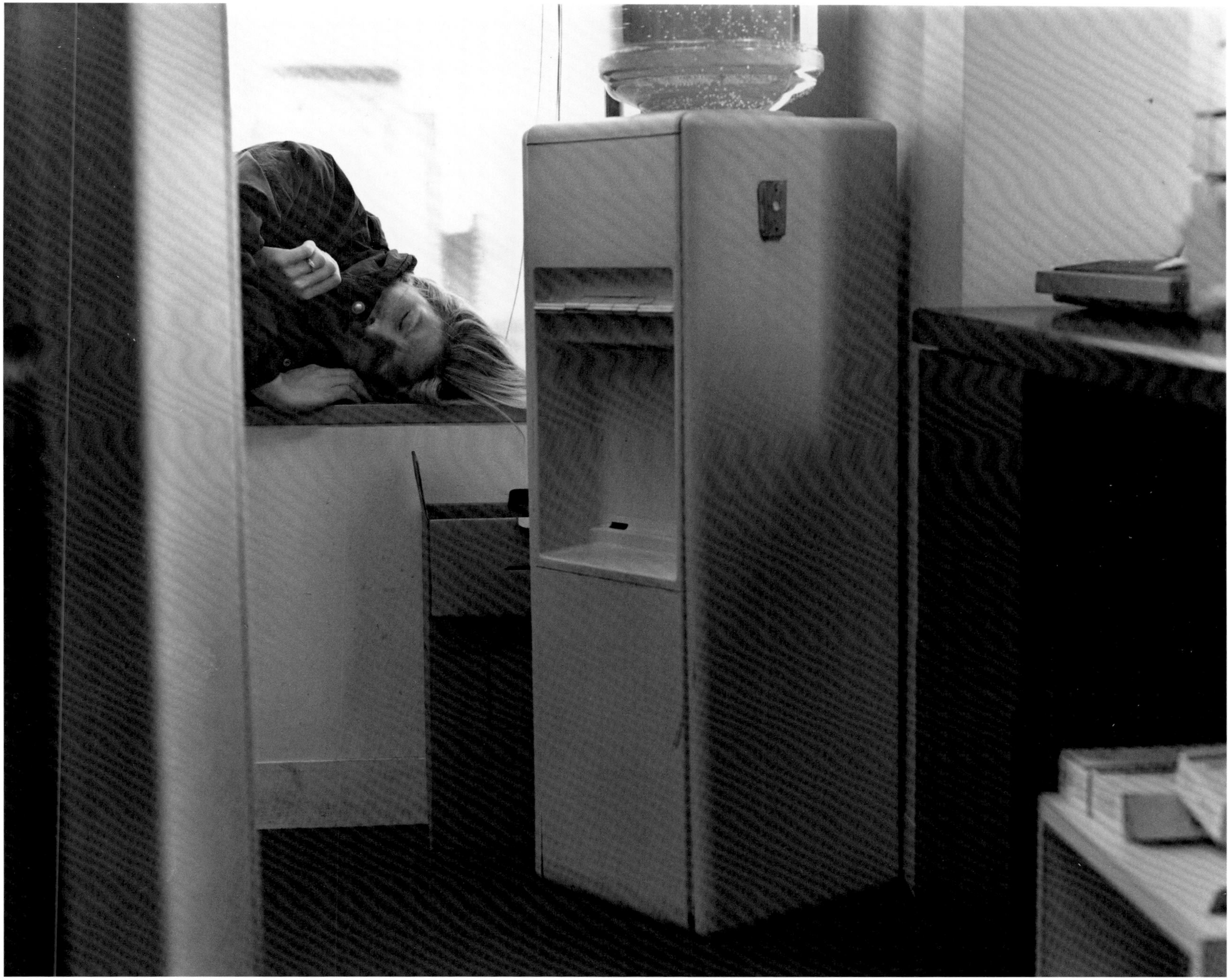

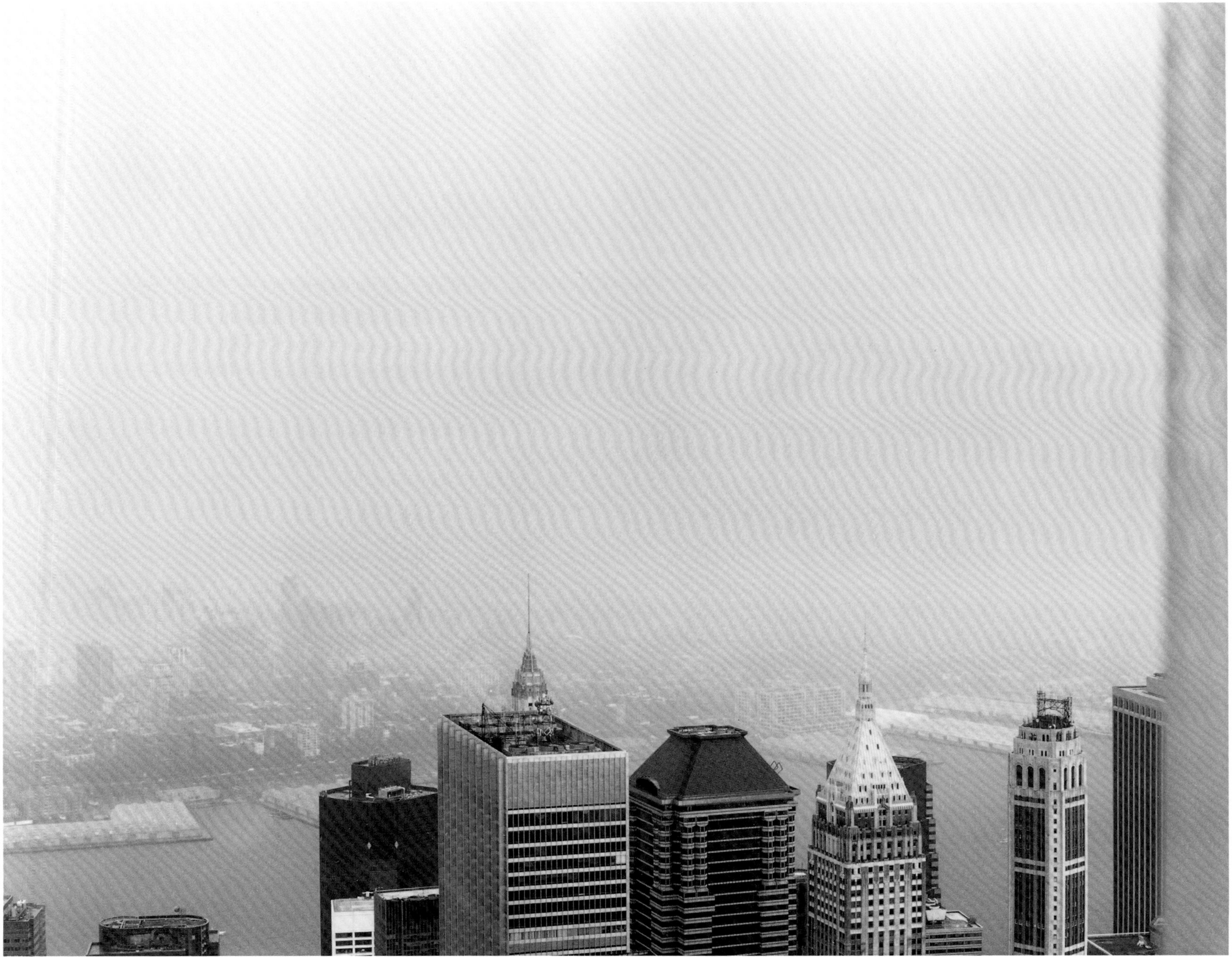

SIREN BEHIND GLASS: ON PILSON'S *INTERREGNA*

Jeffrey Anderson

When we think of photographs of the modern office and its workers, Lee Friedlander comes to mind—the commissioned projects at Cray Computer and The Dreyfus Corporation collected in the book "At Work": a series of formalist exercises, the clean lines of the modern office lingered over, while the workers stare vacantly. . . . With John Pilson's *Interregna*, we are dealing with something different. Like many in New York at the time of the internet bubble, Pilson found himself behind a desk at a large investment bank in the financial district. His shift was the weekend, which meant round-the-clock stints in a powered-down building—a mostly deserted space, half light in the hallways, only one elevator active. What we first see when we look at his photographs from that time are the moments of bleary looking-away—the subjective gaze hovering, dazed, over what happens to be nearby, then expanding out into the trek down the hall to the bathroom, the coffee break, the approach of night, rubbing the eyeballs clean. . . . The title of the work, *Interregna*, means "between the kings" or "between the reigns"—the period where authority is suspended, the few moments before it is reestablished.

As the mention of Friedlander might suggest, we've seen this before, in films even more than photographs—corporate America, the office, the alienation. What is different this time around? First, what we might initially call a *noir* element: not the jagged shafts of light against a living black that is the hallmark of German Expressionism, but a neutral, abstract palette of grays that blurs the usual signposts and captures the vertigo of a place that, like the larger world outside the windows, is very far from anything comfortable or homelike.

For this troubling dimension one of the best references we have is Frederic Jameson's essay on noir icon Raymond Chandler, "The Synoptic Chandler"[1] ("synoptic" echoing the four synoptic gospels, since the first four Chandler novels are the sacred texts of his oeuvre). The *casus belli* of the essay is the puzzle posed by Chandler's third novel, *The High Window* (1942), namely, *why is it not so good?* What's missing from it that the other three books have?

It's not the simplest of questions, given the achievement that these works represent, and Jameson doesn't really address it until halfway through the essay, offering a structuralist analysis of the common elements of our four gospels instead. He sees each of them as a playing-out of the same basic episodes, character types, and tropes, all united under the category of the "office" (for each character, whatever location they are in—home, vacation cottage, hotel, or actual office—functions as an office, preventing other ways of dwelling and being). When each narrative has succeeded in touching these bases, it is complete.

In a feature associated with Balzac's fiction, the environment in Chandler can been seen as expressing directly the essence of the people that dwell in it: e.g., the failed businessman has a dilapidated office, the gigolo a luxury beachfront cottage, the blackmailer the weird sci-fi building he uses for his "psychic consultancy."[2] We can easily throw together an interpretation of Pilson's photographs along these lines: the tired objects that the work includes—hand-exercise balls, fruit, plants, stains, equipment—are in this space the same way that people are: randomly, passively, under duress, bent with the pressure of some unnamed calamity. On this level, *Interregna* seems to be a portrait of the "alienated worker." As Yvonne DeCarlo says in Siodmak's *Criss Cross* (1948), "Keep talking... you make it sound so *nice and sad*."

To go further would be to see the work as the depiction of a human presence that permeates the environment and determines the experiences that can be had within it, blotting out other meanings and thoughts: in this case, the *boss*, who appears in none of the photographs. Up through the 19th century the boss was a decidedly physical presence, since management often involved *beating* subordinates. The contemporary situation is more delicate. In Freud's *Totem and Taboo*, the sons band together and kill their father to free themselves from his oppression, only to find afterwards that the dead father is now omnipresent, a vengeful spirit that must be placated. The presence of the boss has now likewise receded into the background of the office, where, at the edge of vision, it hovers, functioning as the decider of fate and well-being, and must be warded off (being fired is one of the most significant and most hidden experiences in American society). This points up the "transgressive" aspect of Pilson's photographs, which were taken while he was supposed to be working. They lay claim to small pieces of the office. The subjective gaze of the camera denies the totally human environment, since paranoia puts meaning everywhere; instead our attention turns to our screensaver, to an arm hanging over a divider, a jumble of wires, to things that provide us with the relief of the arbitrary, the whimsical and nonsensical.

It is possible, however, to go further than the "systematic" interpretations we have offered so far. Jameson locates the flaw in *The High Window* as follows: it lacks the opening within itself of something that "is not part of its semiotic system, but rather lies beyond it and cancels it as such."[3] "The end of a trajectory, a point beyond which neither writer nor character can seem to go, and which marks the end of the road by being somehow beyond it."[4] So then, what is allowed to emerge in the three perfected Chandler novels that does not show itself in *The High Window*? "The insistence of other orders of being or reality. . . . A vaster, absent natural unity beyond this ephemeral set of episodes in punctual human time."[5]

In Heidegger's essay *The Origin of the Work of Art* he posits two elements that go to make up the creative work, elements that are antagonistic without being separate. The first, "world," is somewhat equivalent to the rational public space that we all inhabit, with its meanings, values, purposes, history, and projects. The other, "earth," is more difficult to gloss. It is the nonhuman that the world takes place within, a silent, dark interior that both supports and disrupts "world." World is the significance of the words I am writing, the larger society in which they circulate, the history that provides their context, the artistry that creates and binds the book where they appear; earth is the ink that will fade and the paper that will decay and rot; earth is the undifferentiated humus into which the book will collapse. As the filmmaker Seijun Suzuki said, "Making things is not what counts: the power that destroys them is."[6]

World and earth are not a duality, but more like overlapping regions — a visible, lit space that shifts against a larger dark, from which things emerge and dissolve again. They are not fixed but dynamic, a process; and a successful work of art is one that holds them in their movement and tension, what Heidegger calls (echoing Heraclitus) their "strife." Here the human world "has no grounding or resonance unless it circulates slowly against the rotation of that other, deeper anti-system which is that of earth itself, and which can include space and 'nature' only at the price of transcending them and enveloping them in its own global negation, coupling them with the nonspace of the outer limit, the white wooden barrier at the end of the world."[7] The wooden barrier here being the white fence at the end of the canyon road in *Farewell, My Lovely,* that "is neither symbol nor contingent reality-effect, neither expressive, semiotic, nor social sign . . . as though it somehow spelled out the very end of space itself."[8] What is possible in the artwork in its truth is that world and earth are manifested in their strife in a "blinding simultaneity."[9]

We can apply this immediately to Pilson's work. As we move through his landscape — cubicle, window, human figures, computer screen, carpet, chair — other elements begin to intrude, and the trajectory of this work becomes clear. Instead of repeating motives that echo the meaningless daily grind of the "alienated worker," or the semi-paranoid exaggeration of the boss's area of control (as in, "this building is the Death Star"), the work, as it plays itself out, begins to descend. The underneath turns towards the camera, and we see silhouettes in night windows, stasis, lunar murk. And the meanings—the situations, feelings, histories, understandings, theories—that were contained in our earlier views of these images begin to dissolve. Other feelings, unvoiced, unwelcome, begin to form. The shimmer of dread and fear—things that must be excluded from the place of work—moves out over a nightscape of severed pieces of the world, meanings truncated at both ends.

To take hold of just one of the severed strands: if the people in these photographs ever leave the workspace, where are they (and, by extension, the viewer of these photographs) supposed to go? To a place without capital, without society, without work? That would mean a place without bodies; and perhaps this is the greatest wish.

We have moved from noir to something much harsher. Strangely, this motion is echoed by one of the strongest influences on Pilson's project—the filmmaker Stanley Kubrick. Kubrick's career begins with the noir systems of *Killer's Kiss* and *The Killing* but soon moves beyond them into the literally unique.

In his mature works Kubrick depicts hermetically sealed human worlds. But the *decay* of these systems is his subject; in time, the denied element seeps in from underneath and the capsule dissolves. This process drives the narrative in each case.

Essential for this is the initial removal of the environment from the supposed "larger world." In the final section of *2001: A Space Odyssey*, the astronauts are on a trip to Jupiter that will take years. In *The Shining,* the writer and his family are taking care of a hotel that is unreachable in the winter months, the road is impassable (this point could be made for all the films: basic training in *Full Metal Jacket* and then its unreal Vietnamese city, with nothing in between; the hotel where Humbert sequesters Lolita for the crime of their consummation, and then their various motels; the strange basement cell in *Paths of Glory* where the soldiers await their execution). In each case these are frozen settings for the destruction of the individual. It is this dimension that bleeds into Pilson's work, with the "dead time" of the weekend and late shifts, the unnumbered hours that descend, a deathly woman in a wheelchair moving down the darkened corridors or placed in the unreal light of the elevator lobby, the weighted air and hum of electronics; we are sequestered in a recess, high above ground, where the world outside has receded. Full daylight finally arrives with the conclusion of the episode.

If, with Kubrick, we avoid the limitations of our earlier "systematic" interpretations, it is because here we are exposed to suffering. It permeates the frames, like a siren going off behind thick glass. It is the final rebuke to the language of alienation: in this manufactured, removed environment, *contra* Friedlander, *pro 2001*, the humans are quite happy to be robots; it is the computer that suffers and goes insane. . . .

Kubrick's sinister humor has echoes in Pilson as well—if the photographer that gives us "time lapse" photos of a computer's screen saver is like a filmmaker who wants to accompany a spaceship in flight with a Strauss waltz. But we should add: a "model" spaceship in flight, created with special effects. The documentary aspect of Pilson's images—the fact that what he photographed was determined by where his employer put him and when he was told to be there—gives overtones and a complexity to this work that are separate.

However it is described, as portraying a return of the repressed (where the parts of a person that are pruned to create a "work persona" return), or delivering a social critique (our inability to comprehend and therefore control the influence of work and technology on our lives), or an exercise in wage-slave Dada (a formalist thumbing of one's nose at the Employer/Father), or, as I have tried to establish here, as reaching towards the nonhuman strata upon which all of these levels play out the half-lives of their meanings, Pilson's photographic work has a way of defamiliarizing the issues involved and bringing them before us with a new force.

NOTES

1. Jameson's essay appears in Joan Copjec, ed., *Shades of Noir* (London and New York, 1993).
2. What is more interesting is the Balzac who hears in every human event the drumbeat of money, which occupies the space previously reserved for the divine; the way the environment, which is money, which exists only because of money, activates the humans set within it, exacts worship from them, and articulates their fate.
3. Jameson, p. 52.
4. Ibid., p. 50.
5. Ibid., pp. 46–47.
6. Suzuki is quoted in the John Zorn essay that comes with the Criterion Collection DVD release of Suzuki's 1967 masterpiece, *Branded to Kill.*
7. Jameson, p. 53.
8. Ibid., p. 51.
9. Ibid., p. 50.

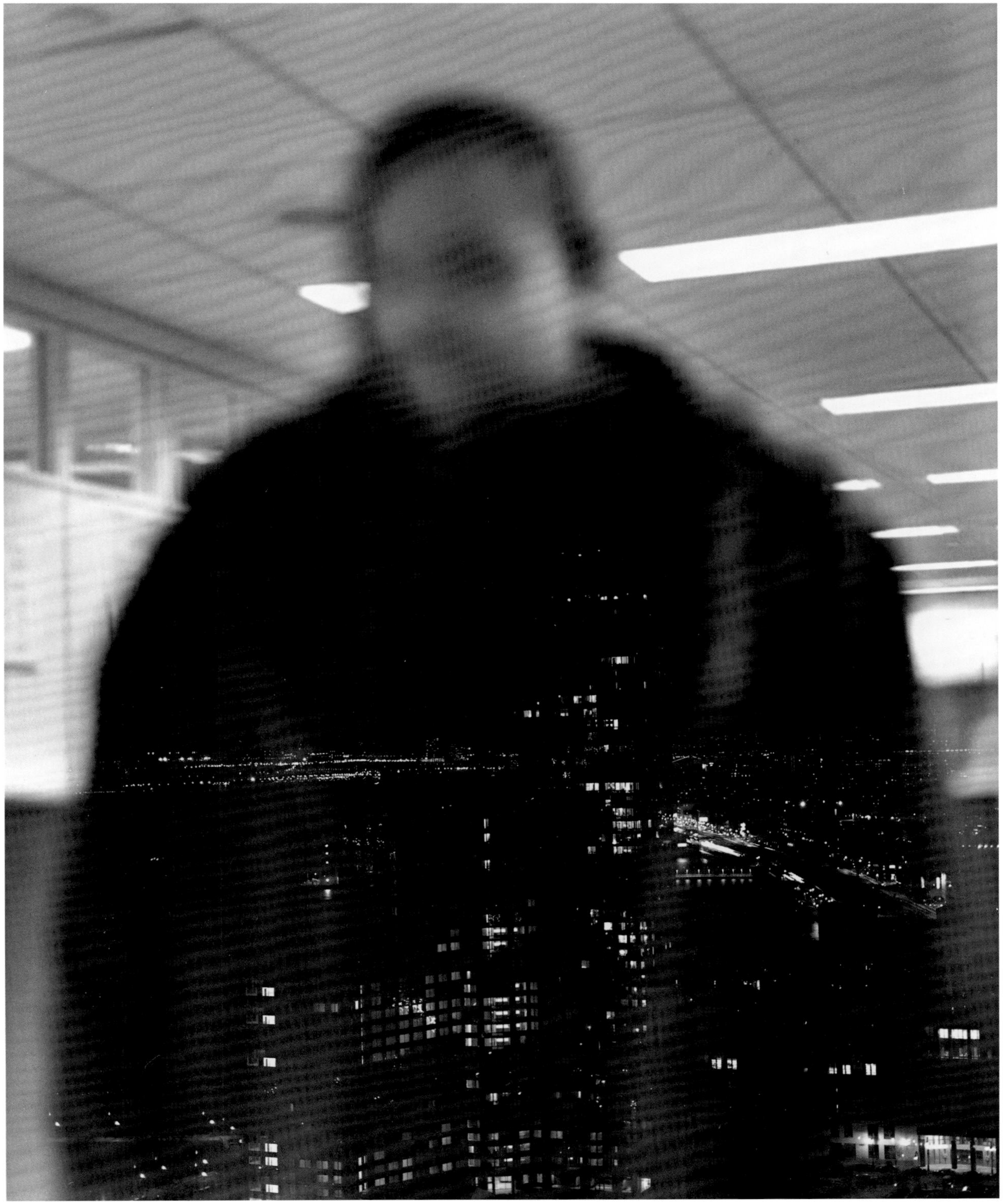

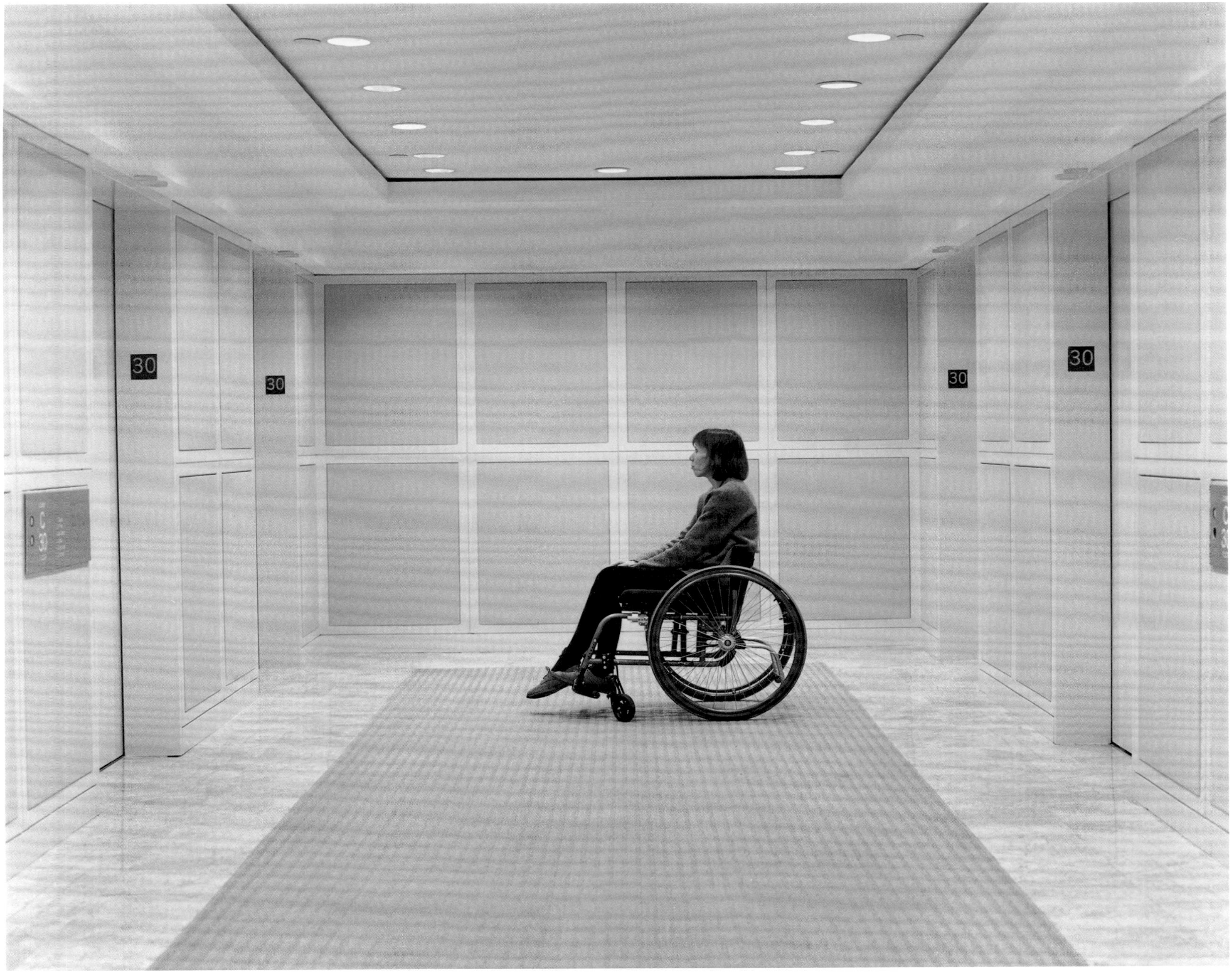
30
30
30
30

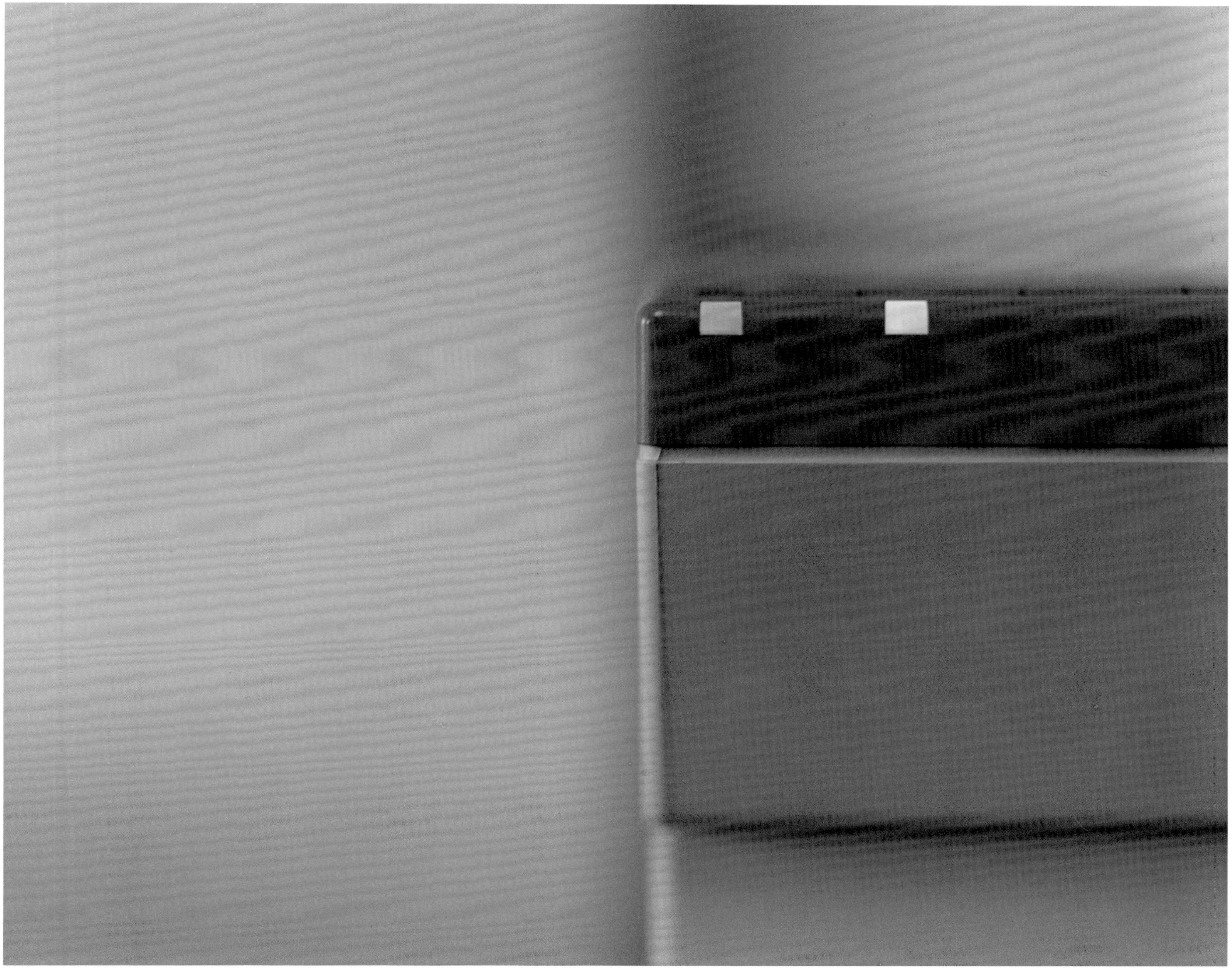

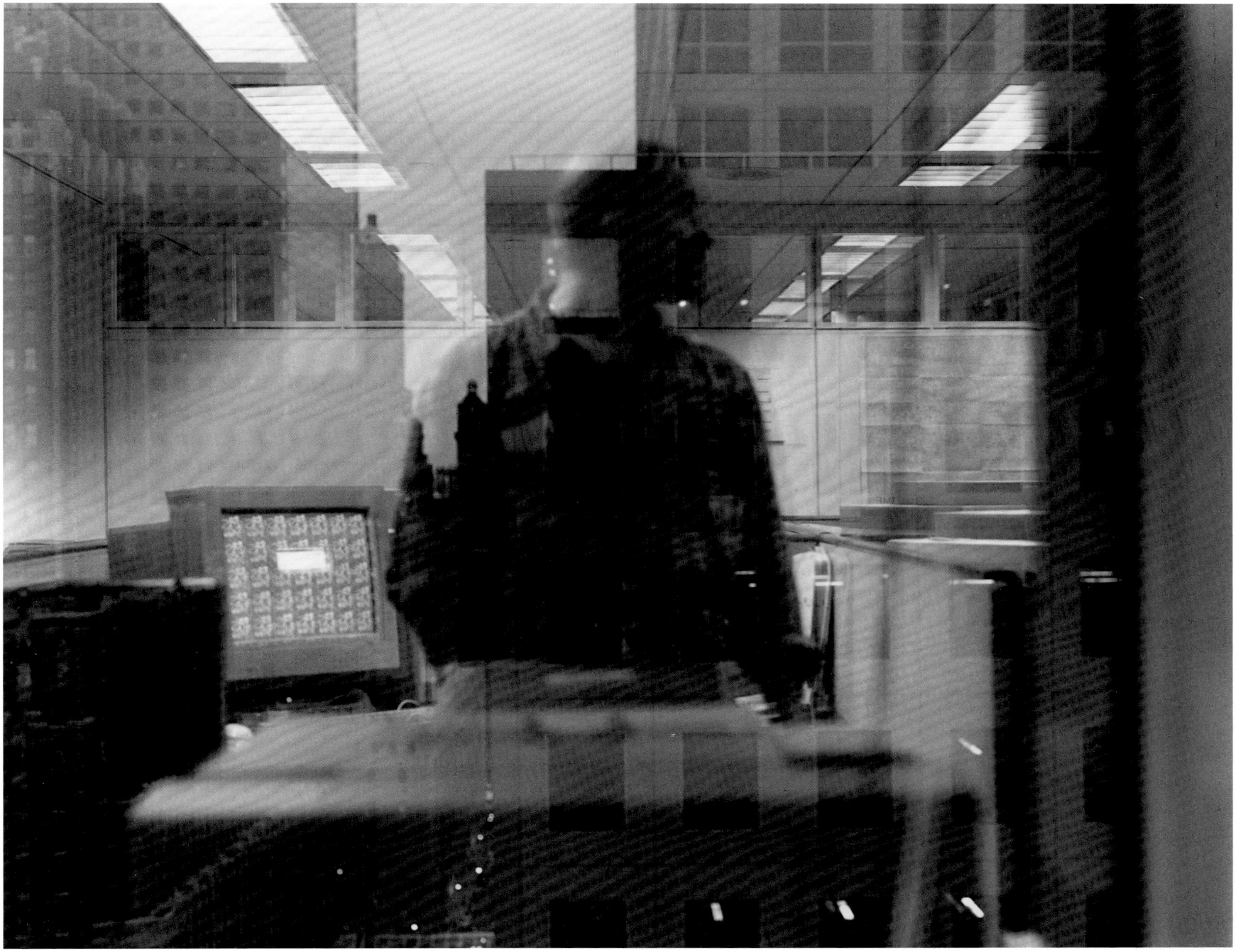

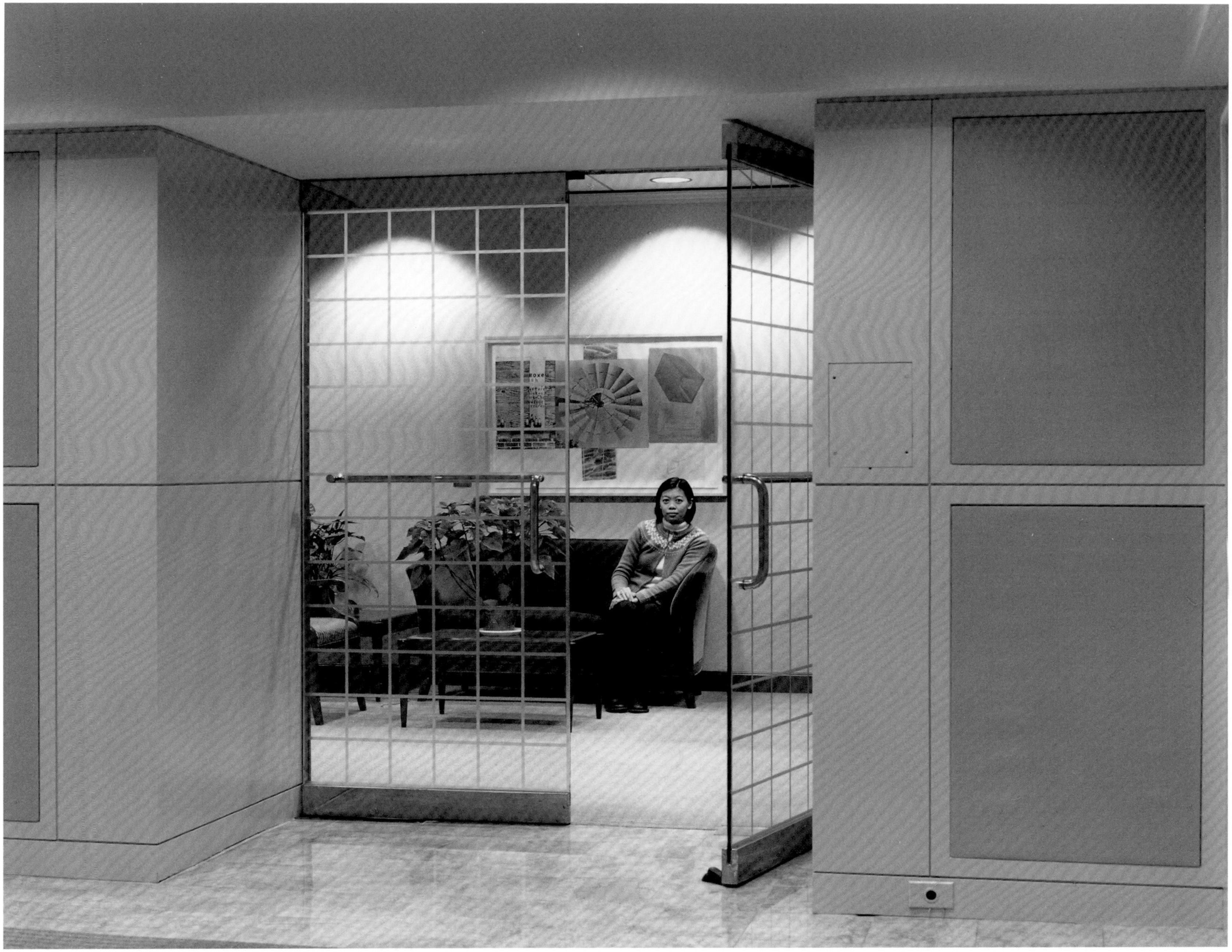

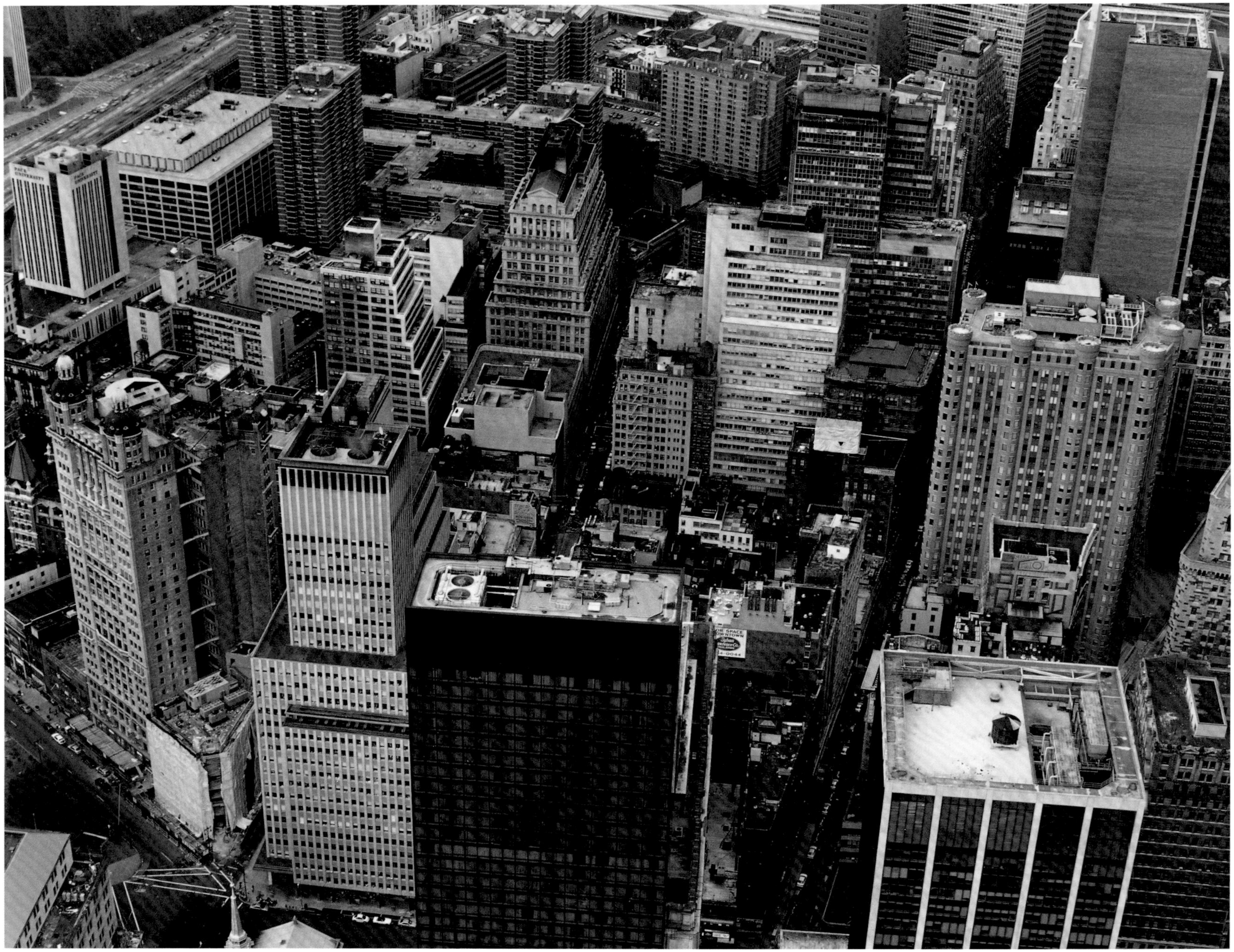

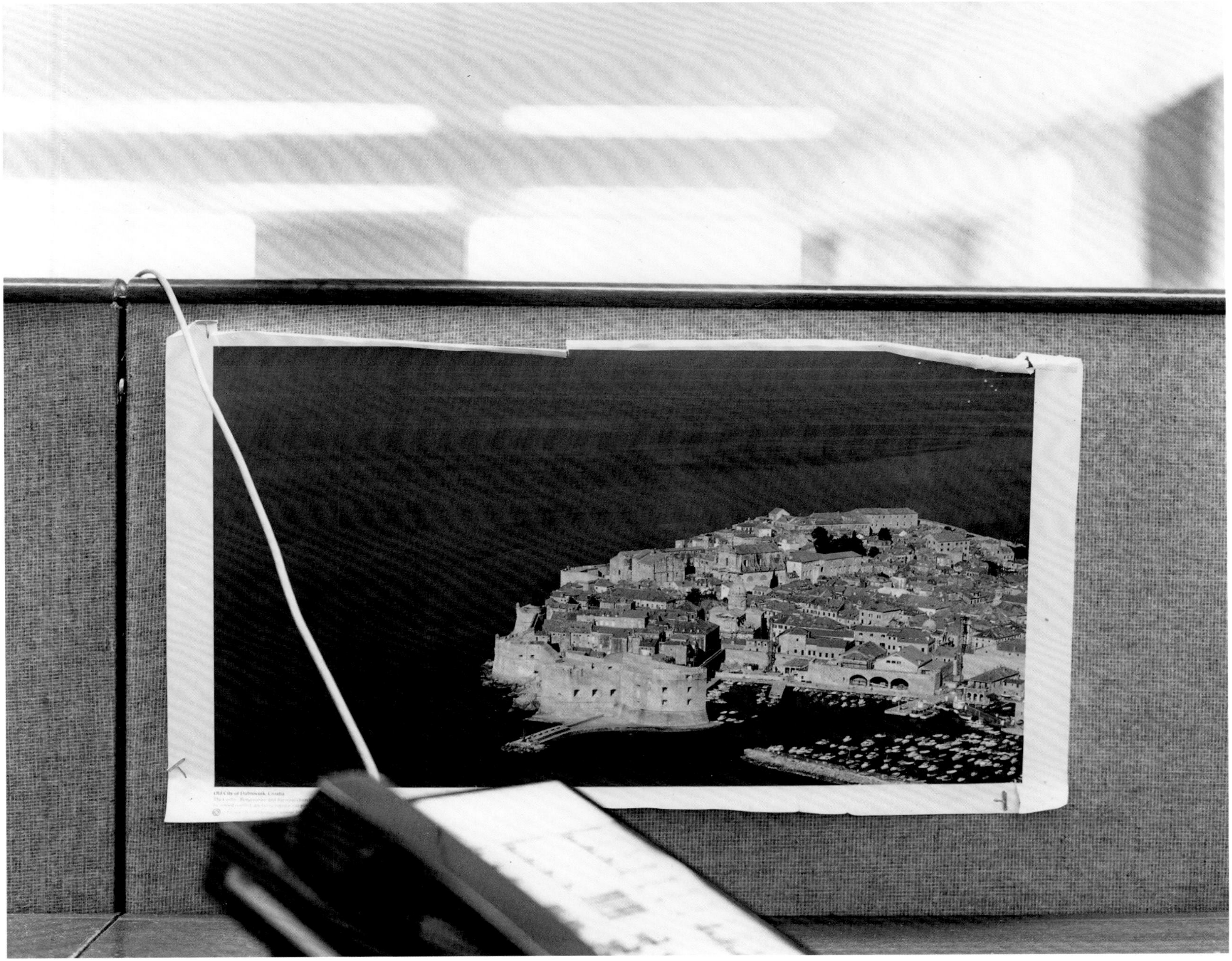
Old City of Dubrovnik, Croatia

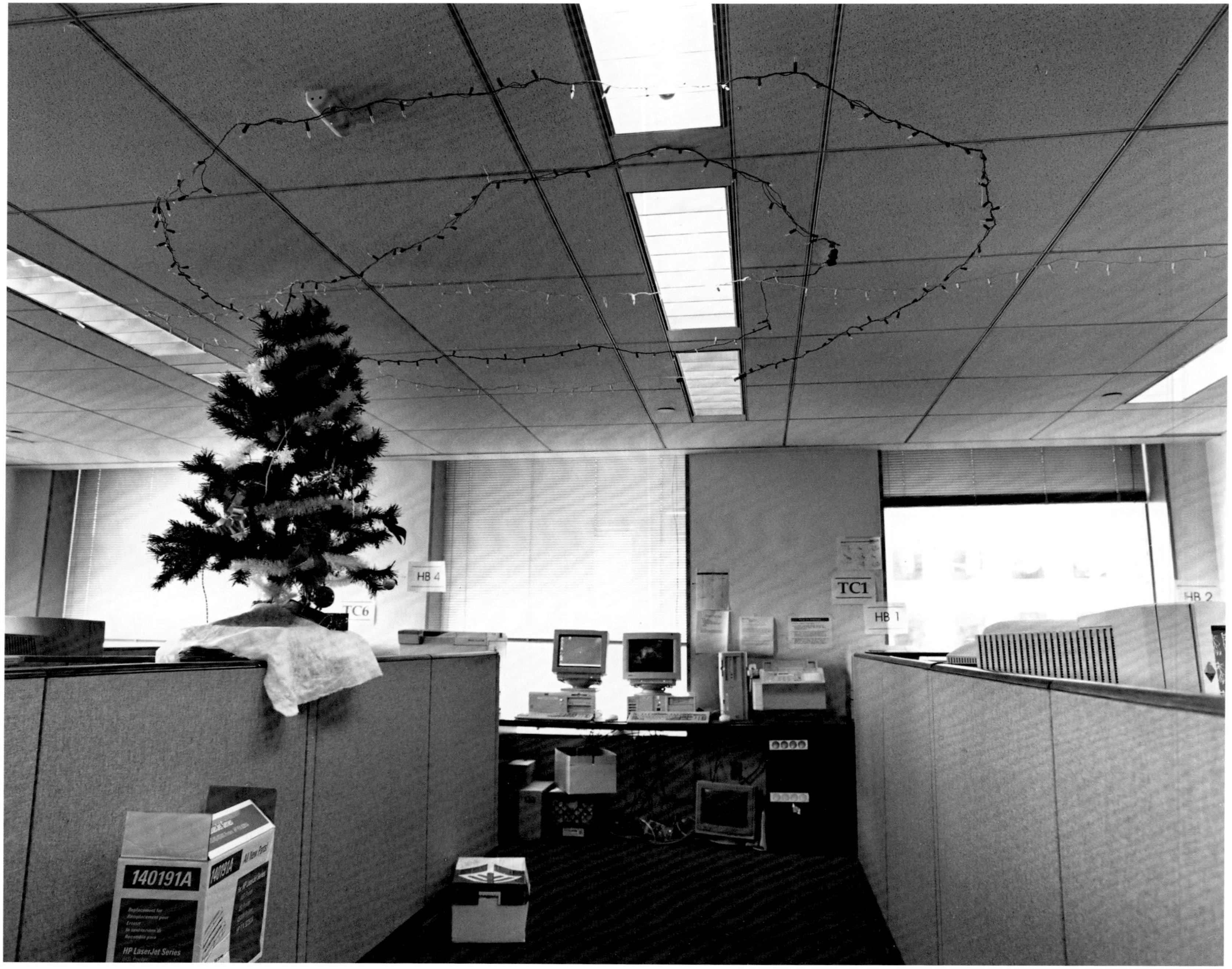
HB 4
TC6
TC1
HB 1
HB 2
140191A
HP LaserJet Series

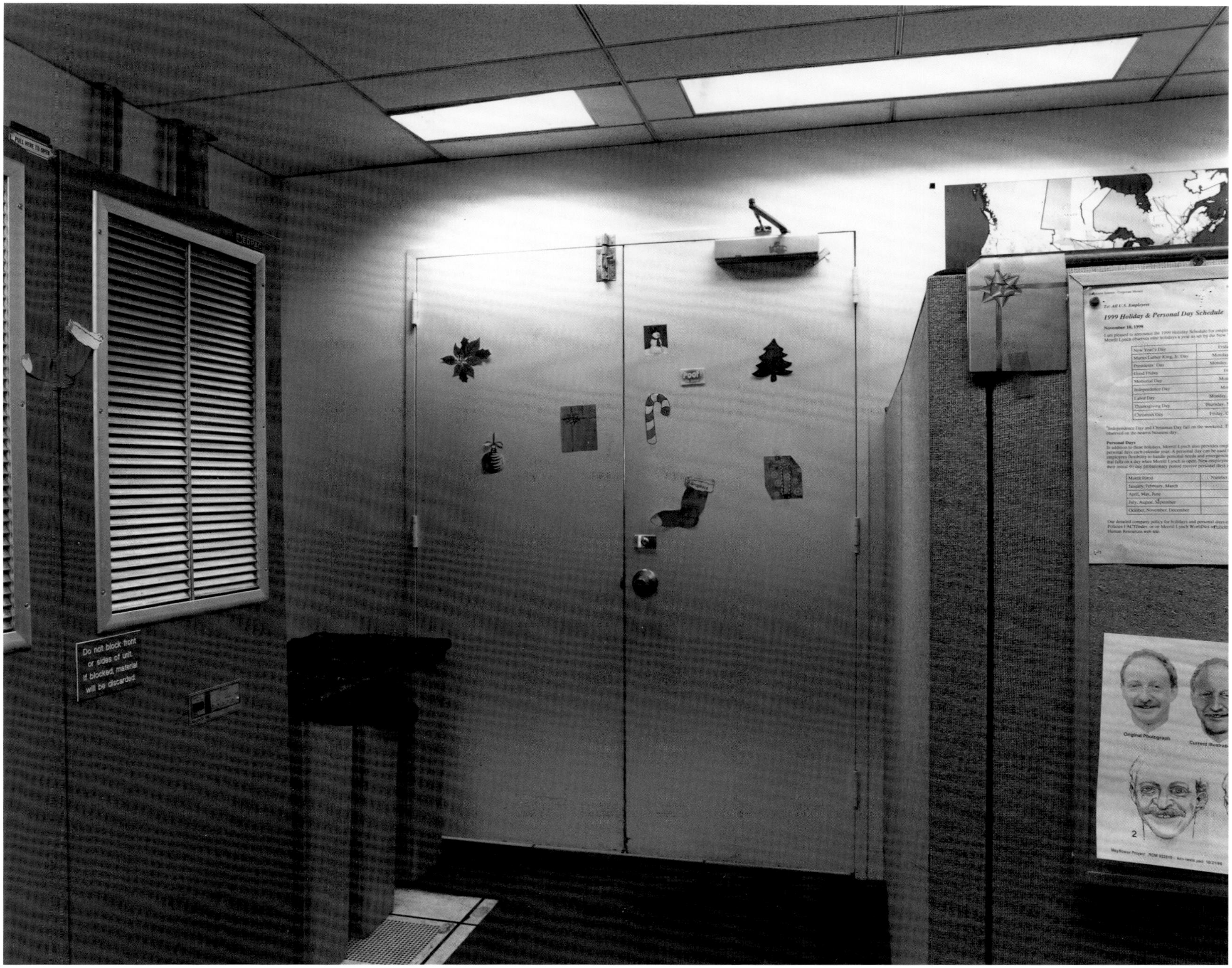

Do not block front
or sides of unit.
If blocked, material
will be discarded.
To: All U.S. Employees
1999 Holiday & Personal Day Schedule
November 10, 1998
New Year's Day
Good Friday
Memorial Day
Independence Day
Labor Day
Thanksgiving Day
Original Photograph

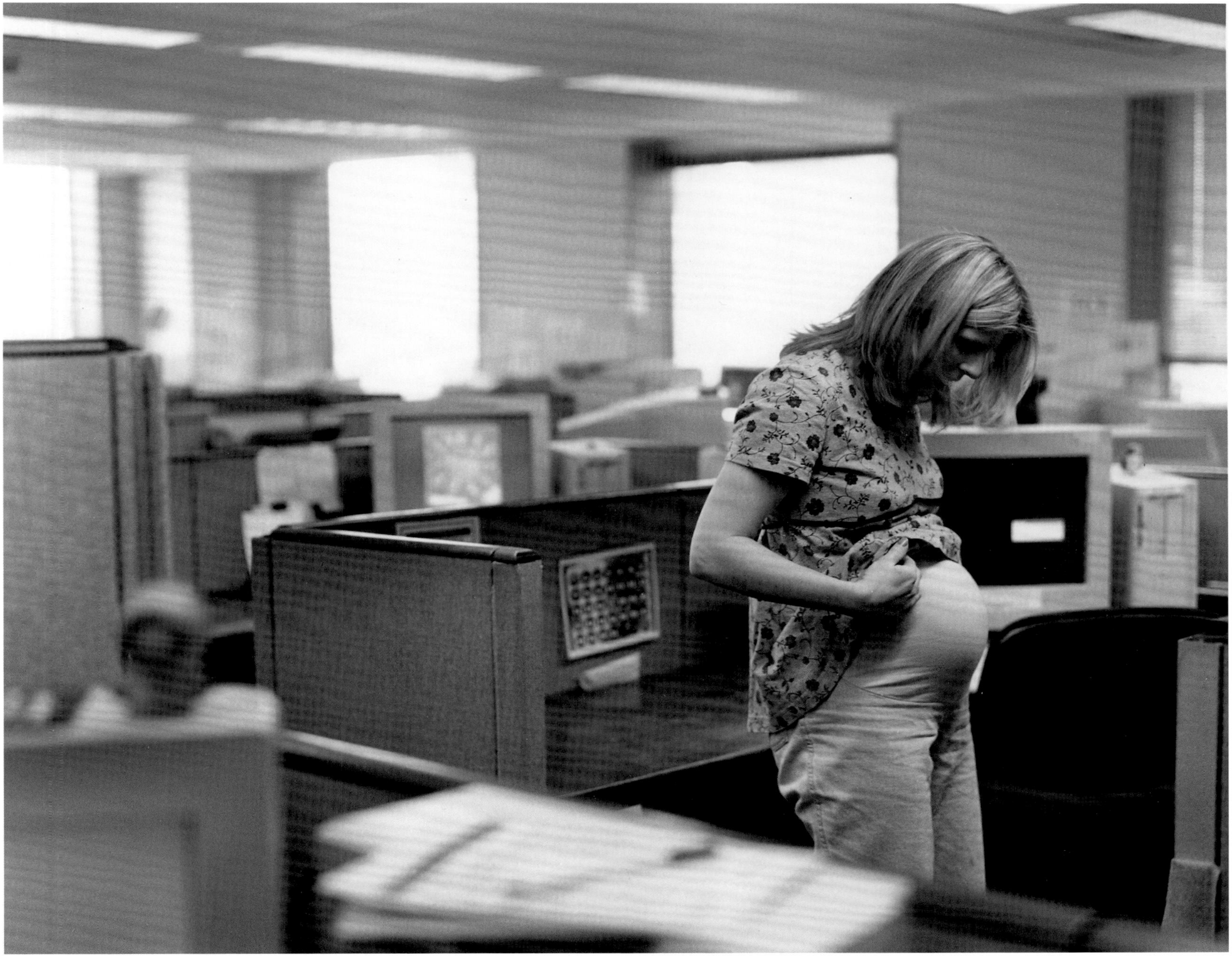

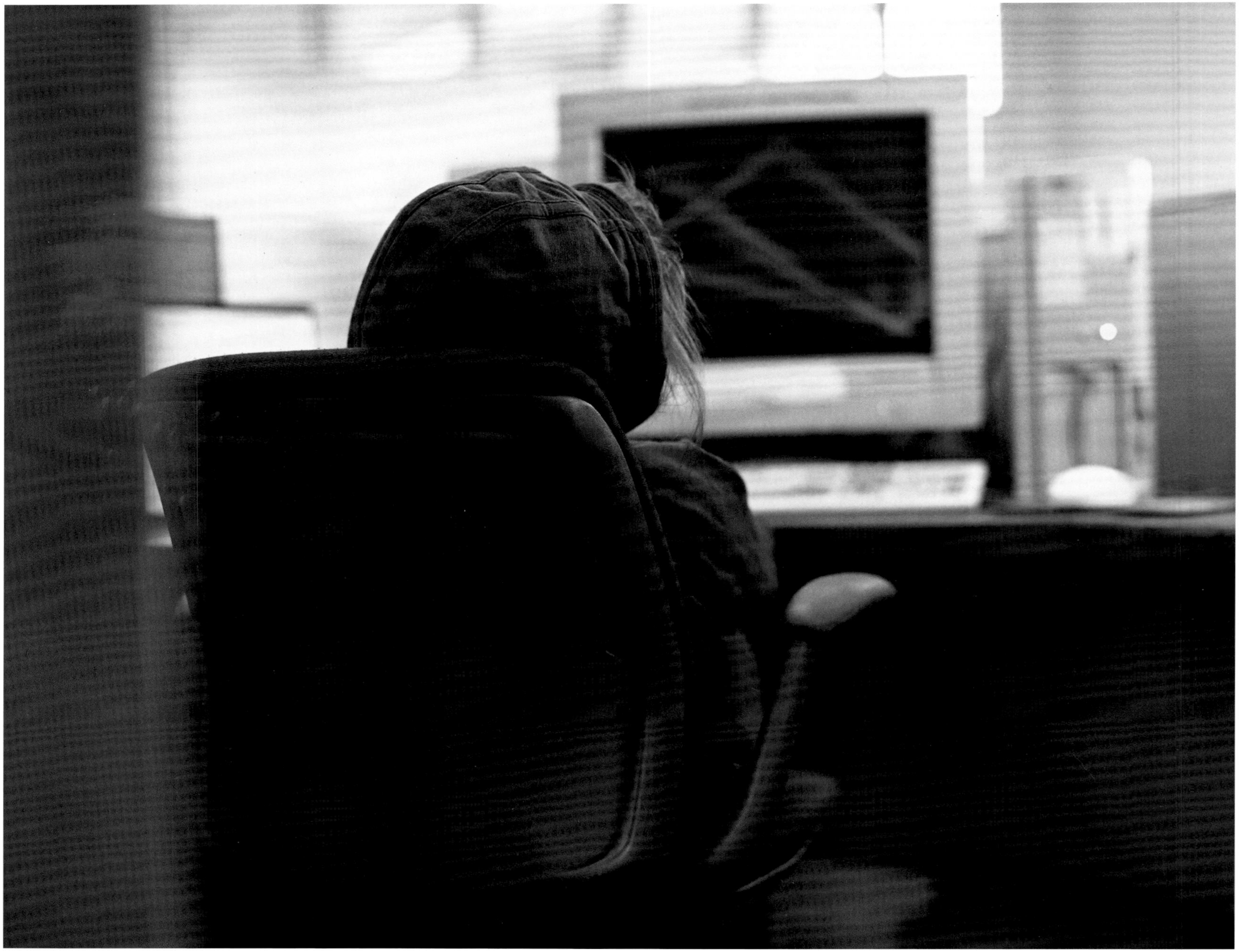

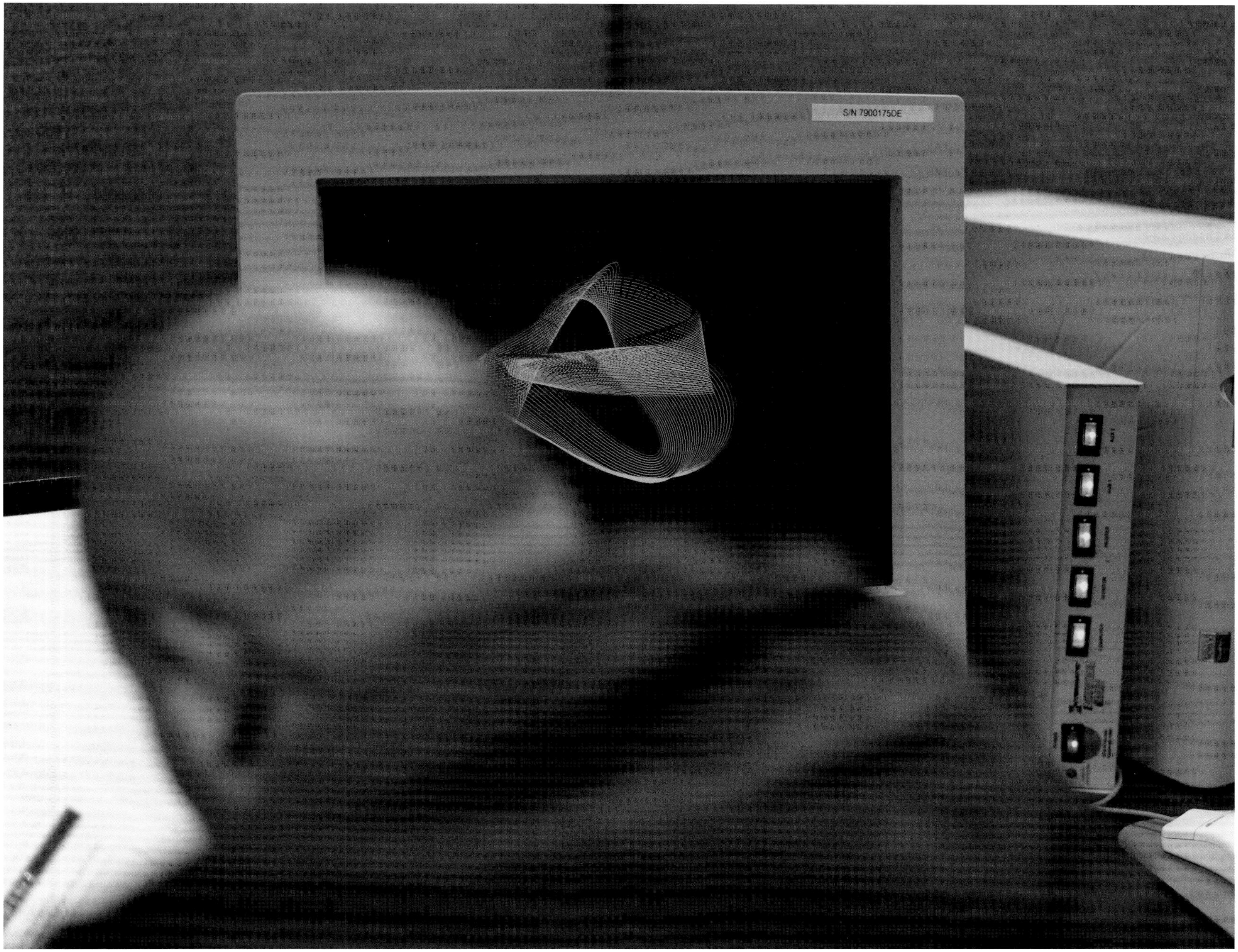
S/N 7900175DE

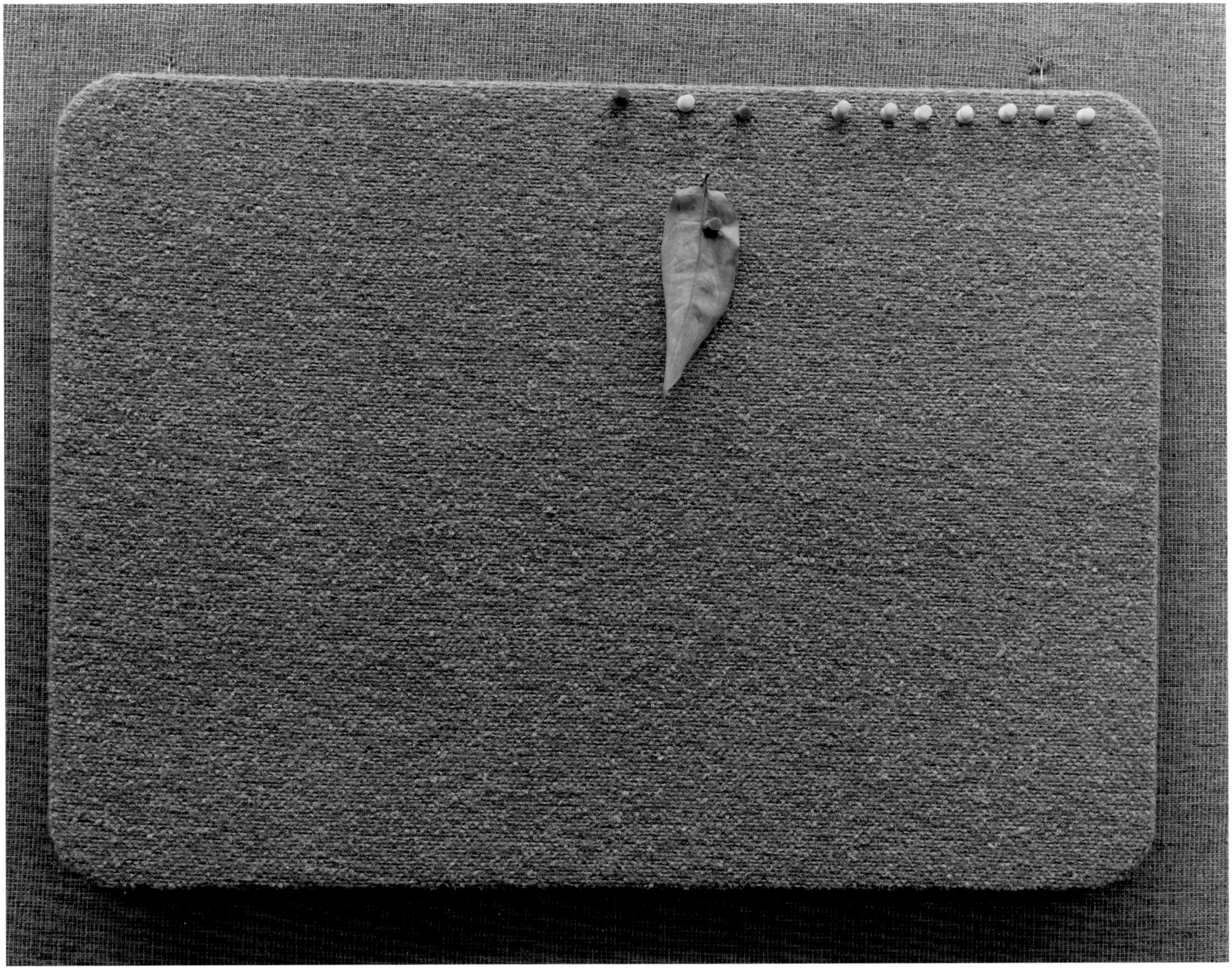

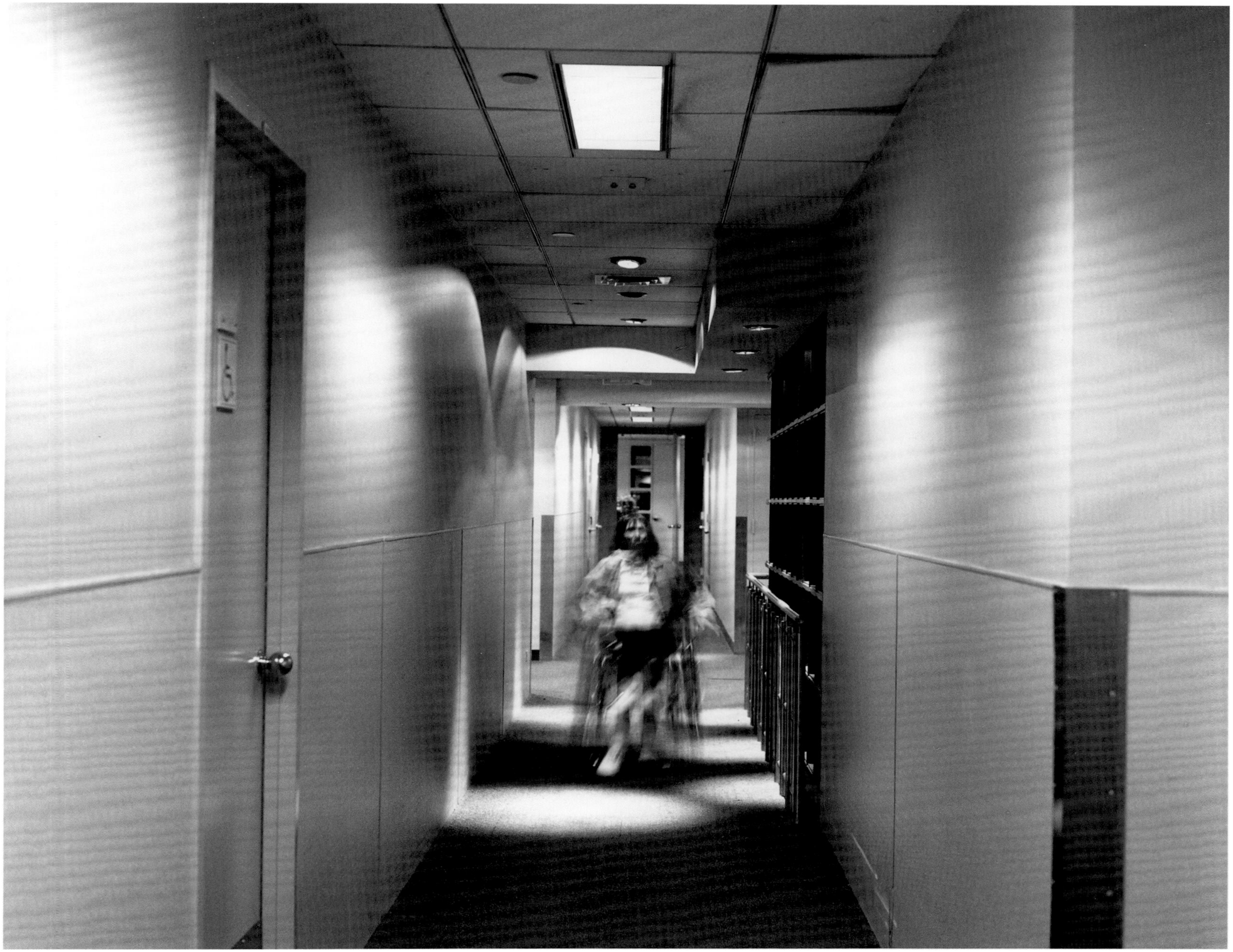

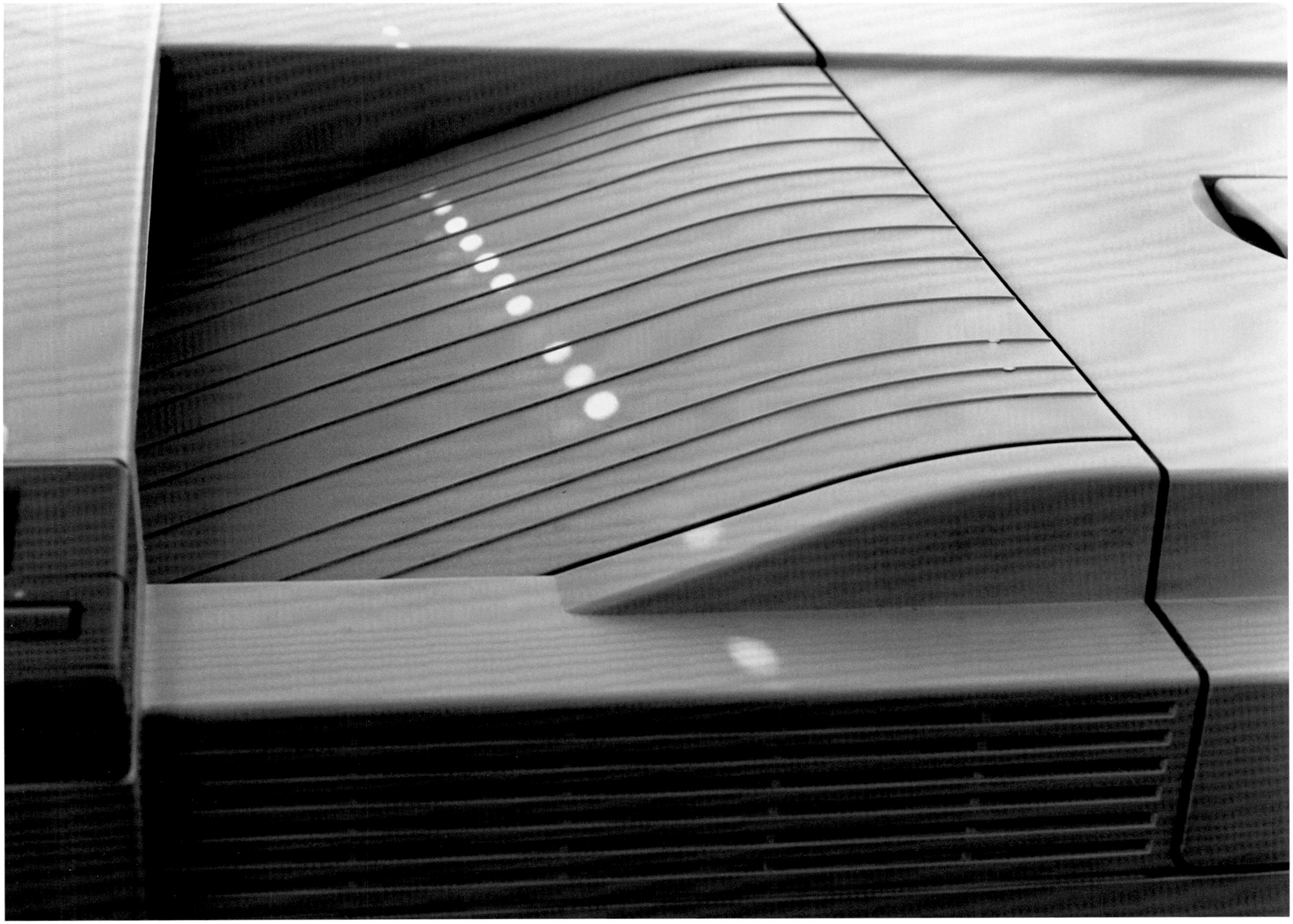

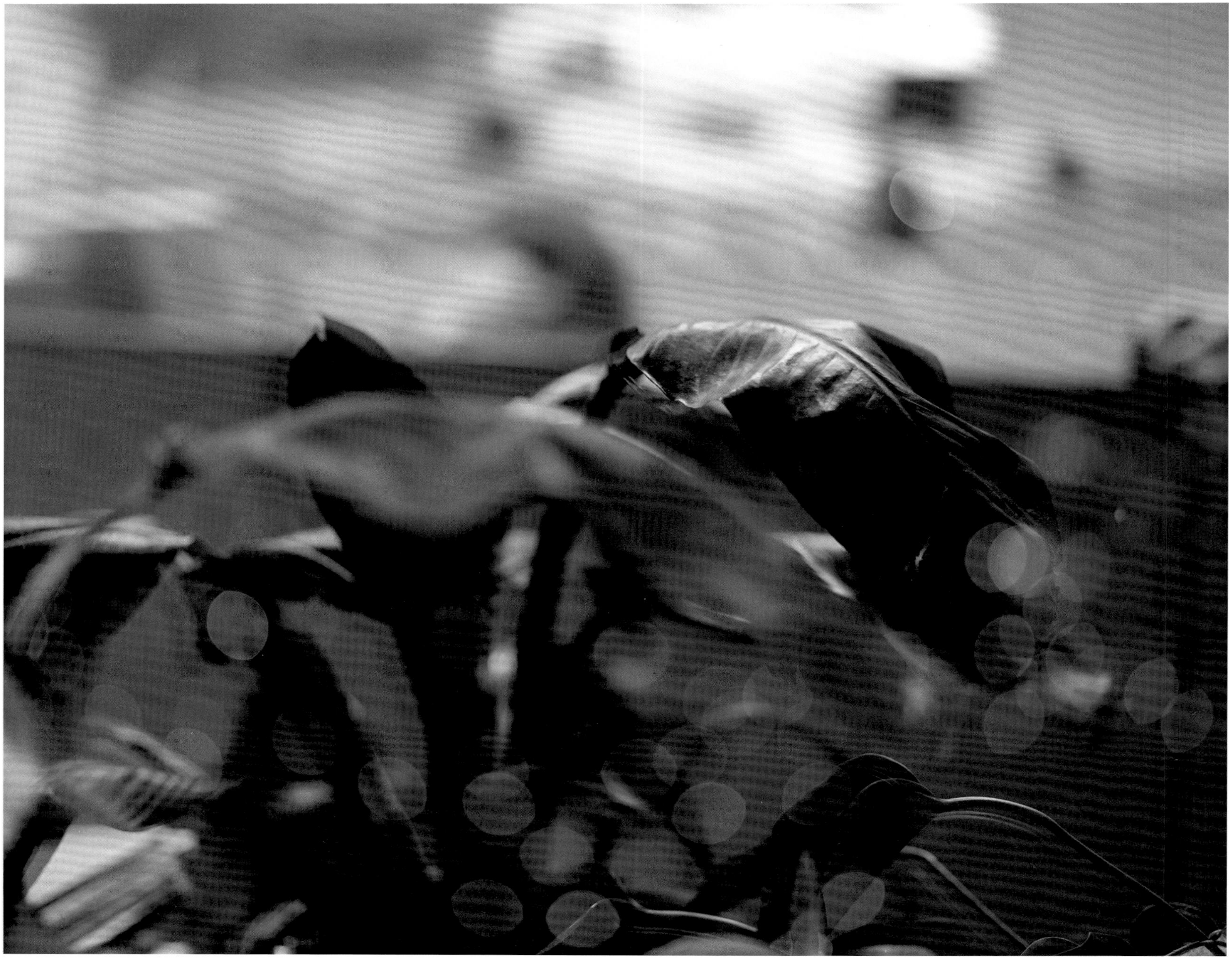

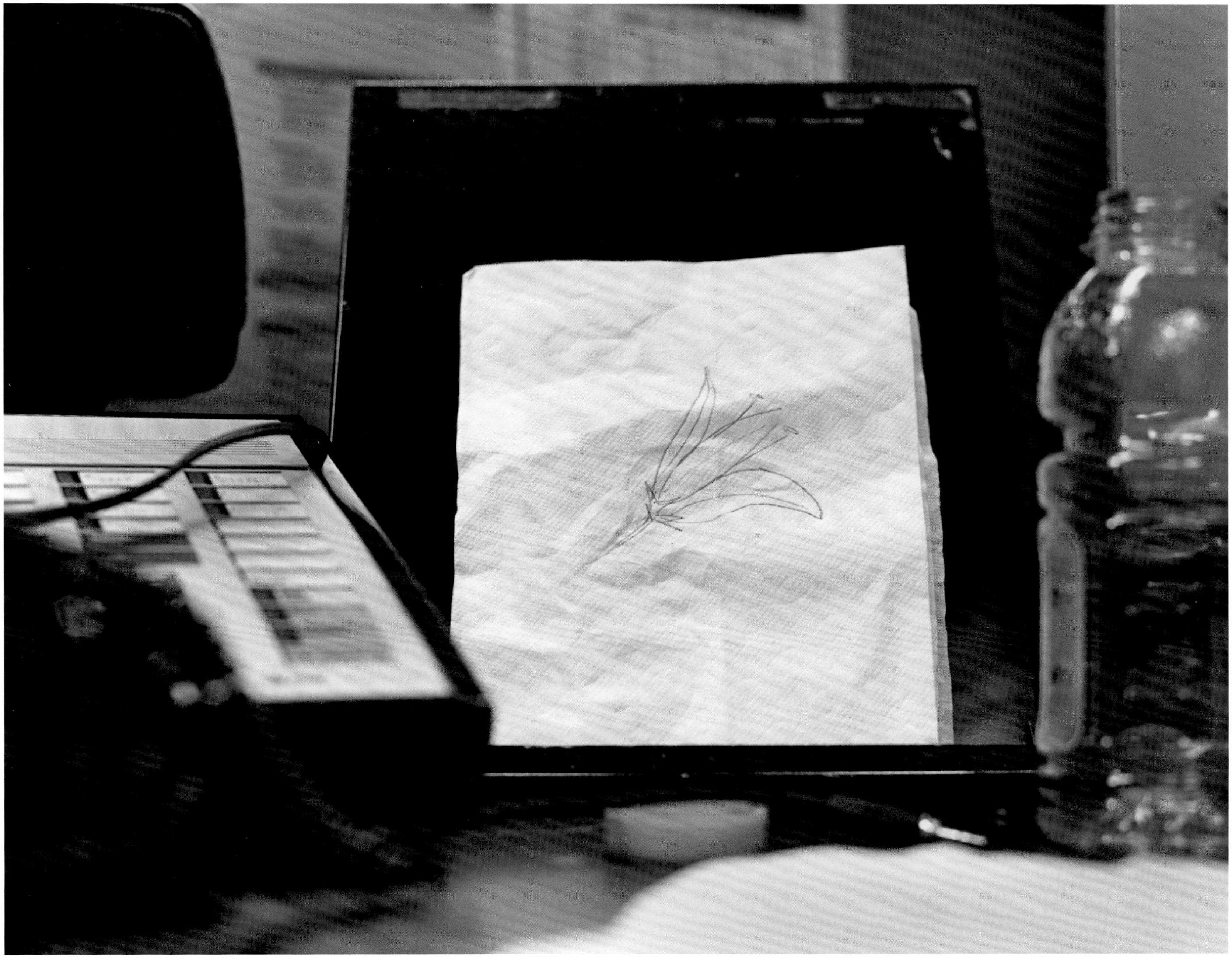

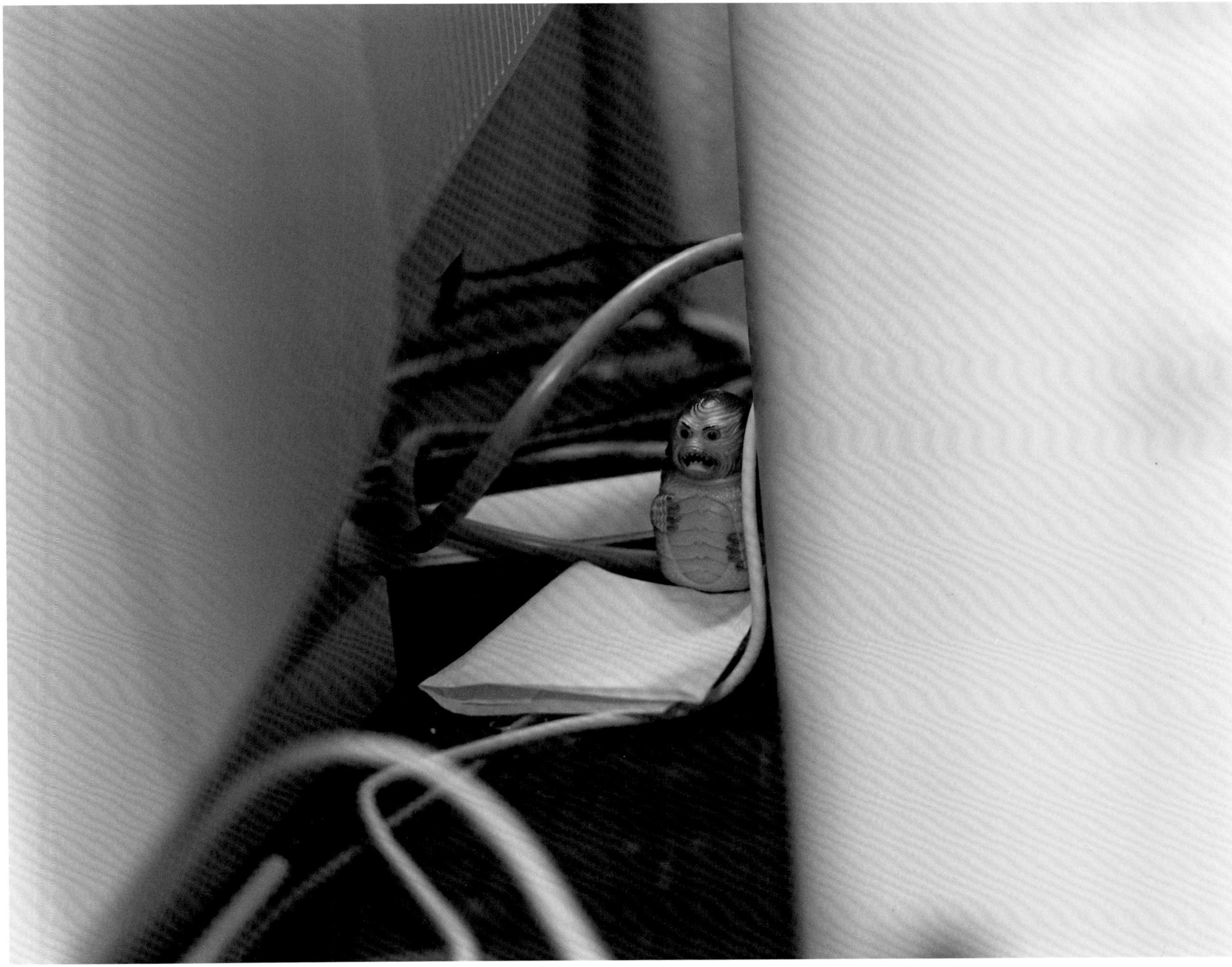

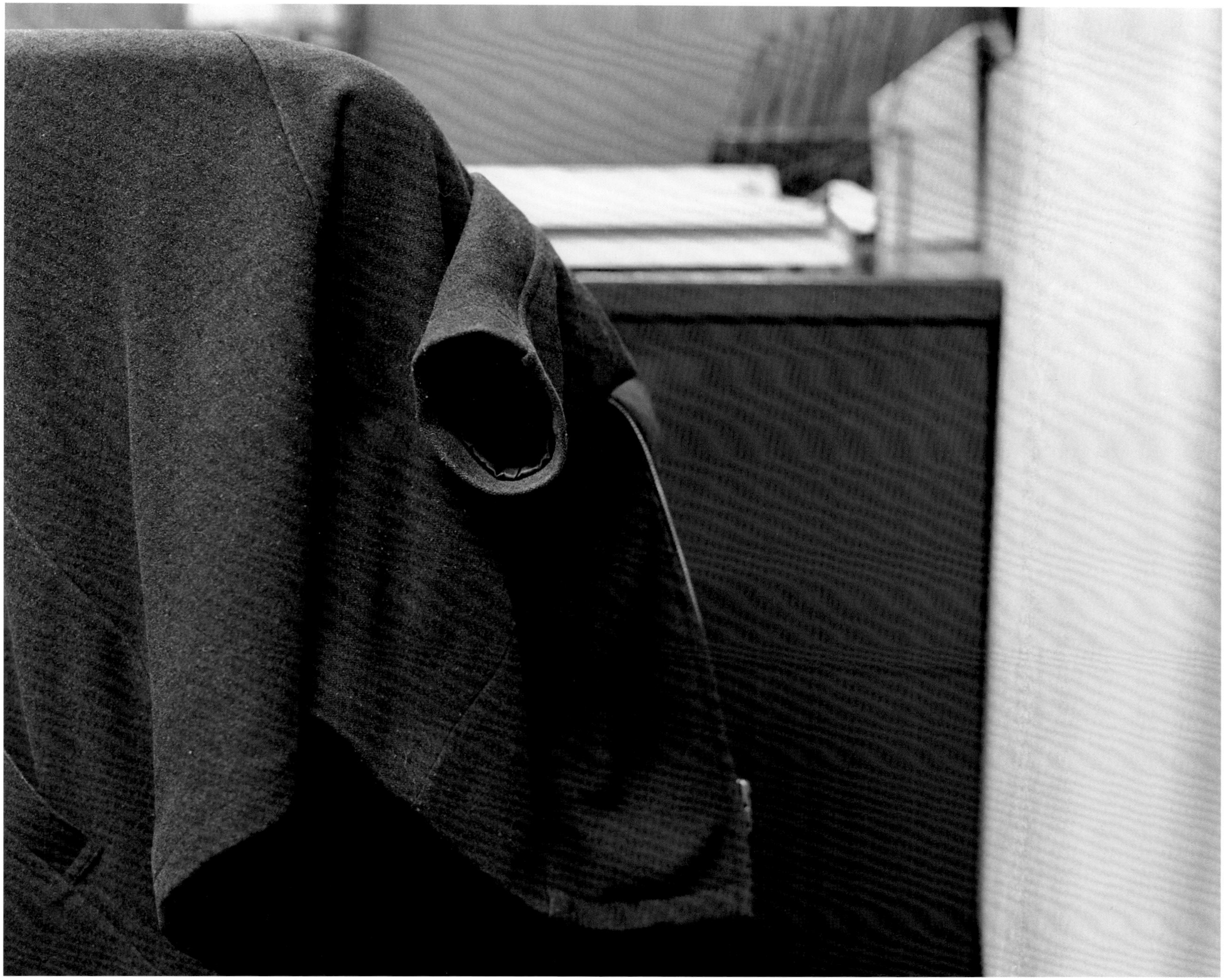

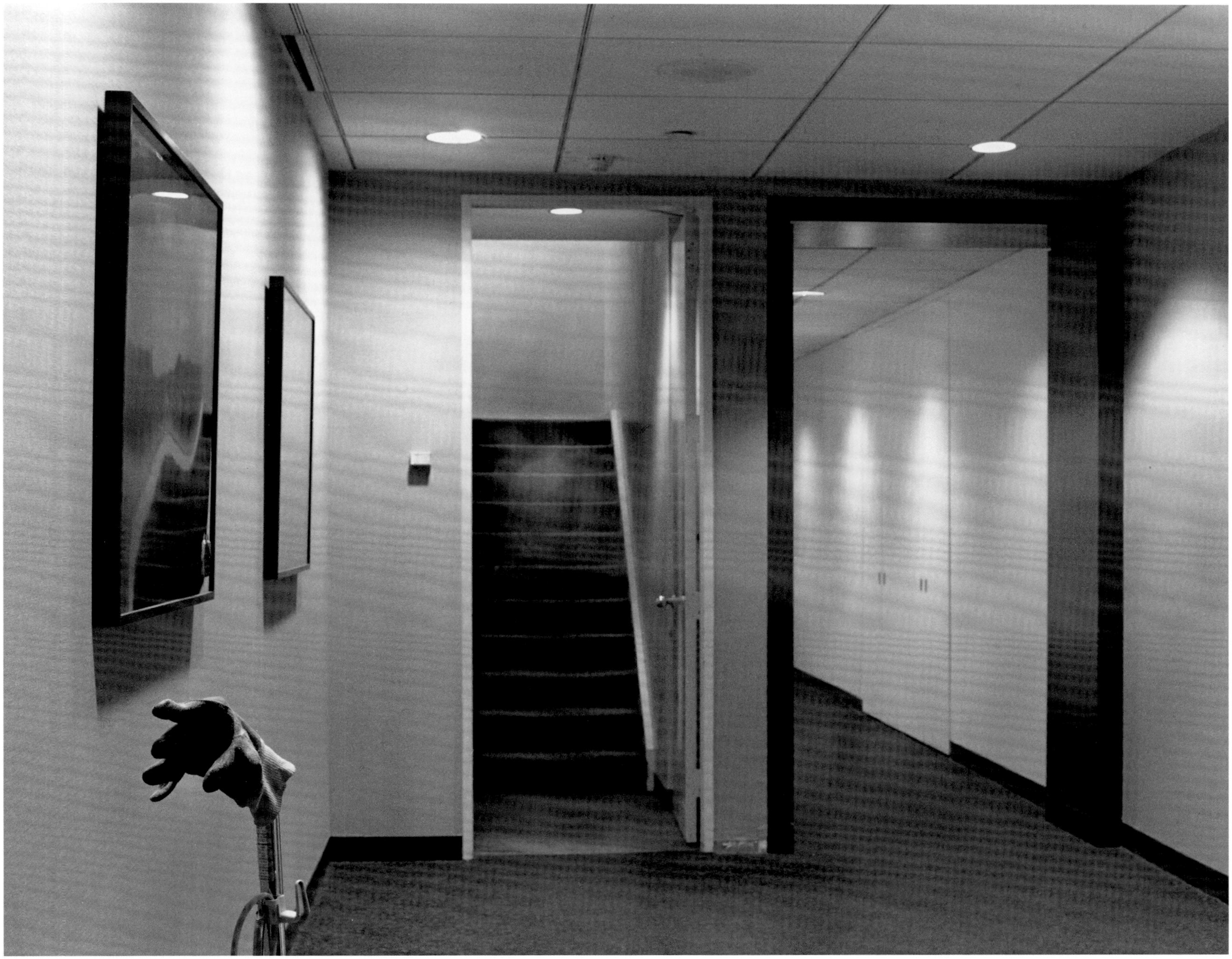

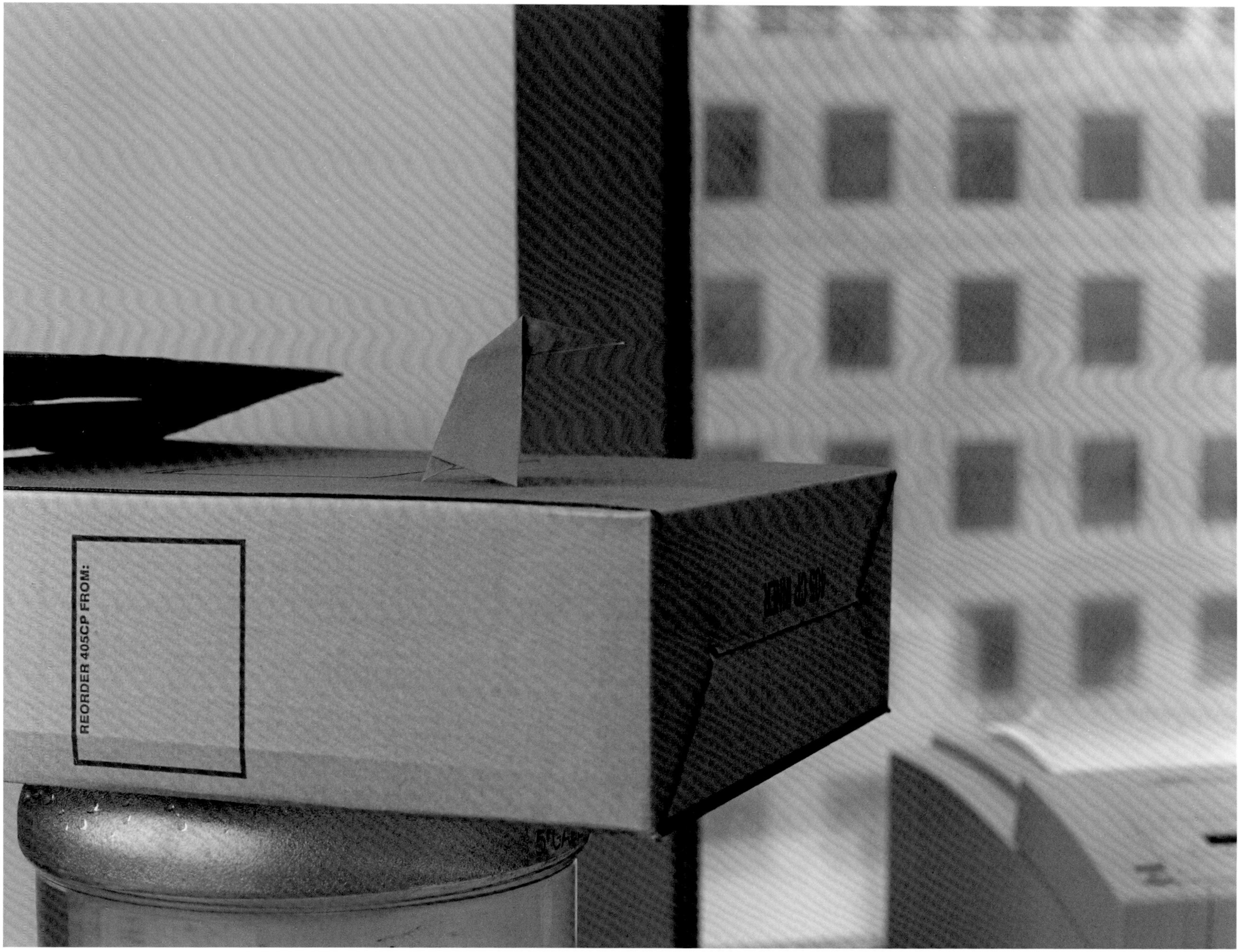
REORDER 405CP FROM:

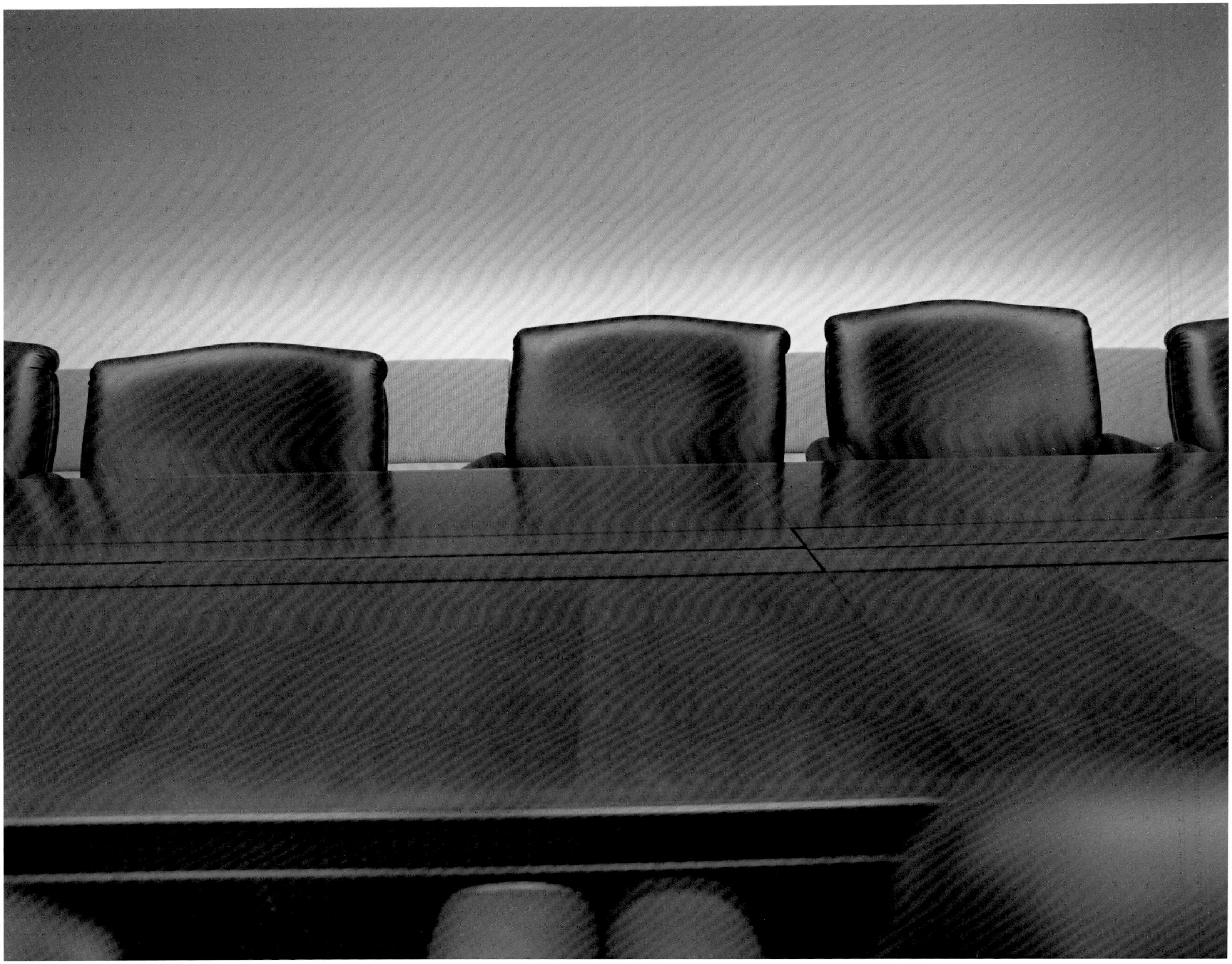

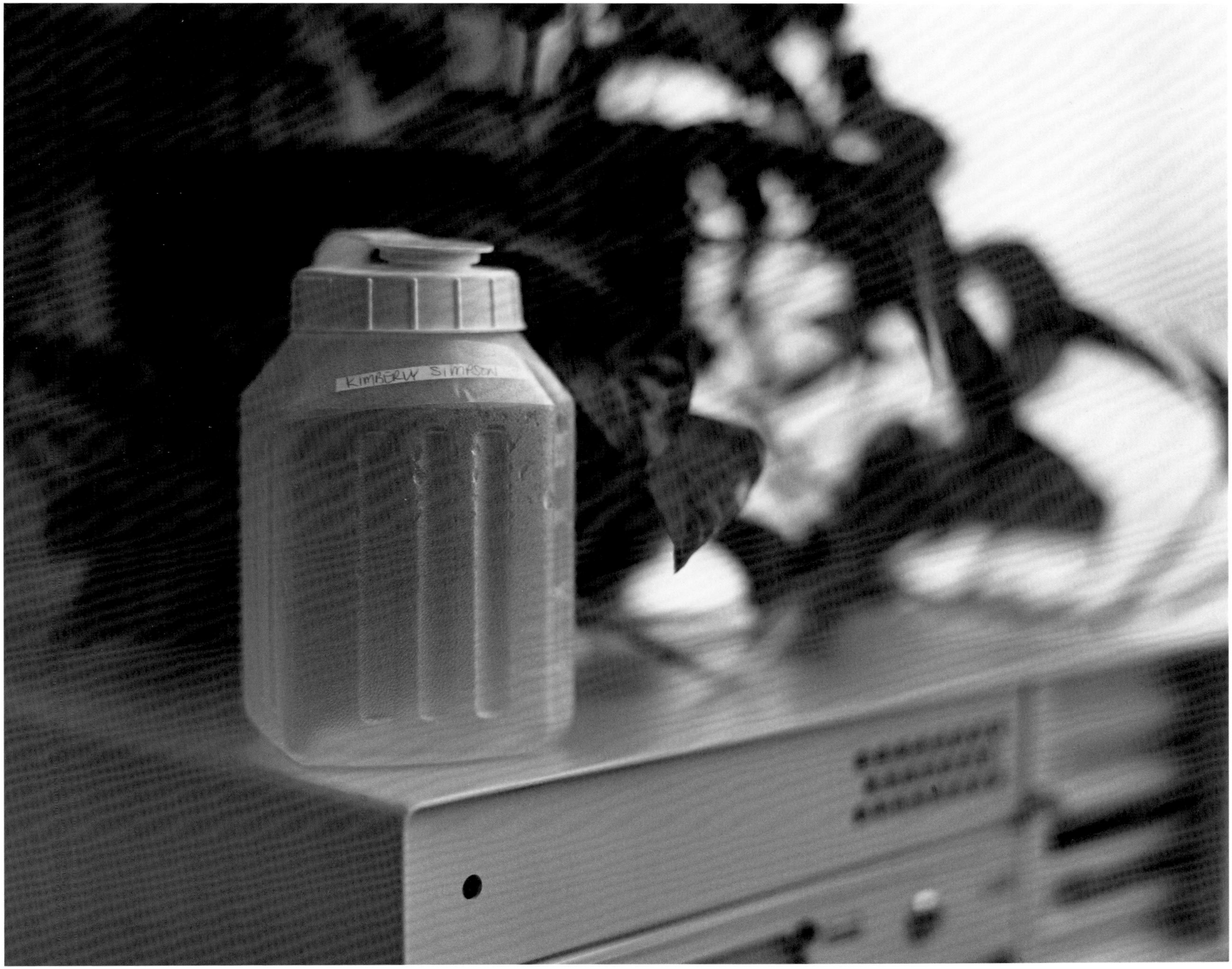
KIMBERLY SIMPSON

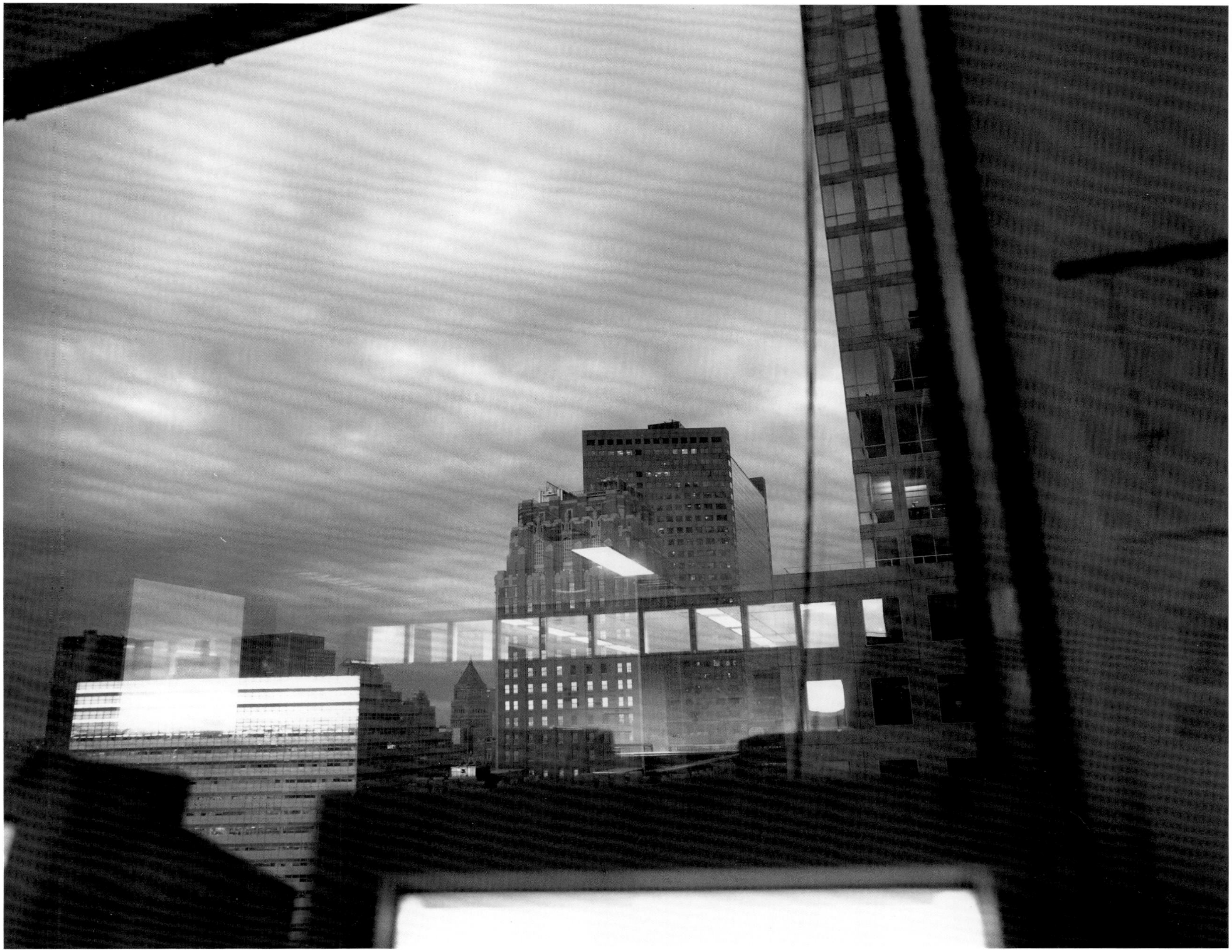

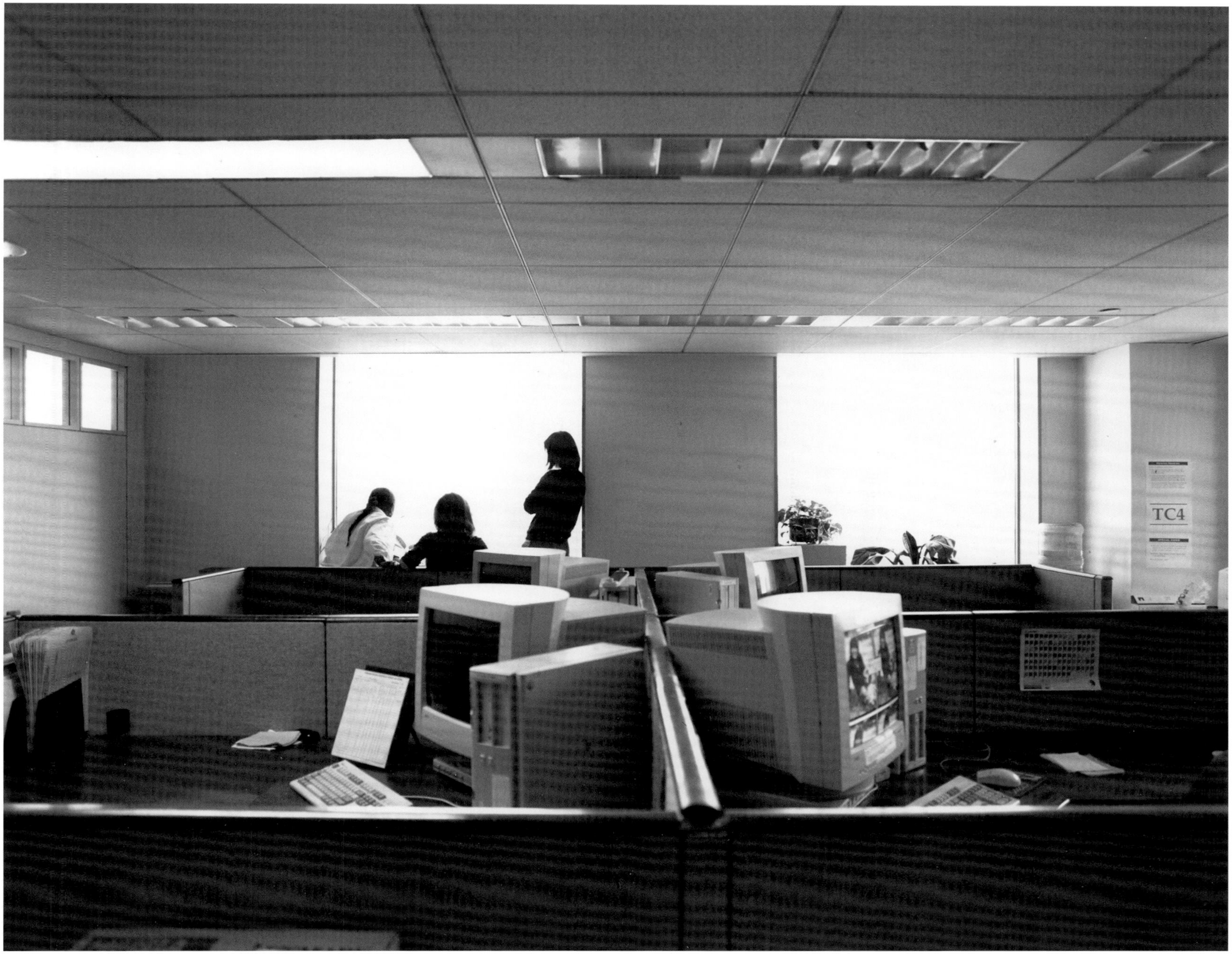
TC4

LIST OF IMAGES

page 41 *Tie and Vent*
Silver Gelatin Print
16 x 20 inches
1998–2000

page 43 *Ramp*
Silver Gelatin Print
16 x 20 inches
1998–2000

page 45 *Dark Corridor*
Silver Gelatin Print
16 x 20 inches
1998–2000

page 47 *Peanut*
Silver Gelatin Print
16 x 20 inches
1998–2000

page 49 *The Archive*
Silver Gelatin Print
16 x 20 inches
1998–2000

page 50 *Palm Tree*
Silver Gelatin Print
16 x 20 inches
1998–2000

page 51 *Two Women*
Silver Gelatin Print
16 x 20 inches
1998–2000

page 53 *ASU*
Silver Gelatin Print
16 x 20 inches
1998–2000

page 55 *New Bag*
Silver Gelatin Print
16 x 20 inches
1998–2000

page 57 *Ball*
Silver Gelatin Print
16 x 20 inches
1998–2000

page 59 *Lunch*
Silver Gelatin Print
16 x 20 inches
1998–2000

page 60 *Corduroys and Armrest*
Silver Gelatin Print
16 x 20 inches
1998–2000

page 61 *Balls and Wire*
Silver Gelatin Print
16 x 20 inches
1998–2000

page 63 *Sleeping Woman*
Silver Gelatin Print
16 x 20 inches
1998–2000

page 65 *City and Fog*
Silver Gelatin Print
16 x 20 inches
2000
From *Above The Grid*

page 75 *C.T.*
Silver Gelatin Print
16 x 20 inches
1998–2000

page 77 *Liz*
Silver Gelatin Print
16 x 20 inches
1998–2000

page 79 *H.P. 1*
Silver Gelatin Print
16 x 20 inches
1998–2000

page 81 *East*
Silver Gelatin Print
16 x 20 inches
1998–2000

page 83 *Lindy in the Waiting Room*
Silver Gelatin Print
16 x 20 inches
1998–2000

page 84 *View*
Silver Gelatin Print
16 x 20 inches
1998–2000

page 85
Dubrovnik
Silver Gelatin Print
16 x 20 inches
1998–2000

page 86
Christmas Spiral
Silver Gelatin Print
16 x 20 inches
1998–2000

page 87
Christmas Door
Silver Gelatin Print
16 x 20 inches
1998–2000

page 89
Maura
Silver Gelatin Print
16 x 20 inches
1998–2000

page 90
Screensaver I
Silver Gelatin Print
16 x 20 inches
1998–2000

page 91
Screensaver II
Silver Gelatin Print
16 x 20 inches
1998–2000

page 93
Bulletin Board
Silver Gelatin Print
16 x 20 inches
1998–2000

page 95
30
Silver Gelatin Print
16 x 20 inches
1998–2000

page 97
T.C. 2
Silver Gelatin Print
16 x 20 inches
1998–2000

page 98
Plants and Lights
Silver Gelatin Print
16 x 20 inches
1998–2000

page 99
Napkin Drawing
Silver Gelatin Print
16 x 20 inches
1998–2000

page 101
Monster
Silver Gelatin Print
16 x 20 inches
1998–2000

page 103
Sleeve
Silver Gelatin Print
16 x 20 inches
1998–2000

page 105
Misty Harbor III
Silver Gelatin Print
20 x 24 inches
2000
From *Misty Harbor*

page 107
Unfinished Origami
Silver Gelatin Print
16 x 20 inches
1998–2000

page 108
Conference Table
Silver Gelatin Print
16 x 20 inches
1998–2000

page 109
Kimberly Simpson
Silver Gelatin Print
16 x 20 inches
1998–2000

page 111
Monitor and Windows
Silver Gelatin Print
16 x 20 inches
1998–2000

page 113
Sunday Morning
Silver Gelatin Print
16 x 20 inches
1998–2000

ACKNOWLEDGMENTS

This book would not have been possible without the fierce support of Nicole Klagsbrun, the critical optimism of Michael Zink, and the unnerving scrutiny of An-My Lê.

The following individuals were essential contributors to this project
and I am grateful to them all:
Liz Garfinkle, Lindy Liao, Maura Beck, Chris Todd, Christine Czarny, Junie Ishimori, Ted Partin, Christine Moog, Stuart Elster, Ruth Paneuf, Daniel Benson, Stephen Shore, Carolyn Ramo, and Jeff Anderson.

Special thanks to Tod Papageorge, Joel Sternfeld, Richard Benson, Lois Conner, Judith Joy Ross, and Susan Kismaric for their definitive lessons and continued friendship.

BIOGRAPHY AND BIBLIOGRAPHY

1968 Born in New York
1991 Bachelor of Fine Arts, Sarah Lawrence College, Bronxville, NY
1993 Master of Fine Arts, Yale School of Art, New Haven, CT

SOLO EXHIBITIONS

2007 Contemporary Arts Center, Cincinnati, OH
2006 *Coliseum*, Nicole Klagsbrun Gallery, New York, NY
2005 *ArtPace*, Hudson Room, San Antonio, TX
Zink and Gegner, Munich, Germany
Western Front Exhibitions, Vancouver, Canada
St. Denis, MW Projects, London, UK
2004 *Dark Empire*, MW Projects, London England
2003 *St. Denis*, Nicole Klagsbrun Gallery, New York, NY
2002 *Clean Lines*, Art Basel 33, Basel, Switzerland
Annet Gelink Gallery, Amsterdam, Netherlands
2001 Nicole Klagsbrun Gallery, New York, NY
John Pilson (Torbjorn Vejvi), Raucci / Santamaria Gallery, Naples, Italy
2000 *Above the Grid*, P.S. 1—Contemporary Art Center, Long Island City, NY

SELECTED GROUP EXHIBITIONS

2006 *Time Frame*, P.S. 1, Long Island City, NY, Curated by Neville Wakefield
The Office: In and Out of the Box, Dorsky Gallery, Long Island City, NY
Modern Time, Work, Machineries and Automation in the Arts of 1900, Palazzo Ducale, Genoa, Italy, Curated by Germano Celant
The Rhubarb Society, Tracy Lawrence Gallery, Vancouver, BC
SLAPstick, Lora Reynolds Gallery, Austin, TX, Curated by Christopher Eamon
Nothing but Pleasure, BAWAG Foundation, Vienna, Austria

2005 *A Kind of Portraiture*, Art Basel Miami Beach—Art Video Lounge, Program #10, Curated by Christopher Eamon
Predatory Dating On The Crosstown Bus, A New York Kind of Disappointment, A Special Kind, Champion Fine Art, Los Angeles, CA, Curated by Guy Richards Smit
Office Hours, Neue Gesellschaft für Bildende Kunst, Berlin, Germany
Paper, Nicole Klagsbrun Gallery, New York
Premieres, Museum of Modern Art's Department of Film and Media, New York, NY

2004 *Simulation City*, Centre Pour L'Image Contemporaine, Geneva, Switzerland
MoMA The Museum of Modern Art Modern Means: Continuity and Change in Art from 1880 to Present, Mori Art Museum, Tokyo, Japan

2003 *Altered Spaces: Video Art and the Physical World*, Cheekwood Museum of Art, Nashville, TN
The Moderns, Castello di Rivoli, Museo d'Arte Contemporanea, Rivoli, Italy*

2002 *Moving Pictures*, Solomon R. Guggenheim Museum, New York, NY
Copy, Roth Horowitz, New York, NY

Sudden Glory: Sight Gags and Slapstick in Contemporary Art, California College of Arts and Crafts, Wattis Institute of Contemporary Art, Oakland, CA*

Interior/Exterior, Nicole Klagsbrun Gallery, New York, NY

2001 *Bureaucracy*, Foksal Gallery Foundation, Warsaw, Poland

Loop—Alles auf Anfang, Kunsthalle der Hypo-Kulturstiftung, Munich, Germany, Travels to P.S. 1 Contemporary Art Center, Long Island City, NY*

The Americans—New Art, Barbican Gallery, London, England*

Video Jam, Palm Beach Institute of Contemporary Art, Lake Worth, FL

49th International Exhibition of Art, Plateau of Mankind, Venice Biennale, Italy*

World Without Ground, Chase/Freedman Gallery, West Hartford, CT

Ghosty, 1000 Eventi Gallery, Milan, Italy

2000 *Some New Minds*, P.S. 1—Contemporary Art Center, Long Island City, NY

Moma2000: Open Ends, The Museum of Modern Art, NY

The City, Nicole Klagsbrun Gallery, New York, NY

Greater New York, P.S. 1 Contemporary Art Center, NY*

Shockwave, Raucci/Santamaria Gallery, Naples, Italy

Work, 312 Gallery, Chicago

Kunst-Werke, Berlin

1998 *Citizens*, New York Public Library, NY

1997 V*isionaires*, Museum of Contemporary Art, Los Angeles, CA

SELECTED BIBLIOGRAPHY

2006 "Laura Kleger and John Pilson," (interview) *North Drive Press* #3

Wilson, Michael, "John Pilson: Nicole Klagsbrun Gallery," *Artforum*, May

Schwendener, Martha, "John Pilson," *Time Out New York*, March 30–April 5

Ross, Christine, "The Aesthetics of Disengagement; Contemporary Art and Depression", University of Minnesota Press, Minneapolis, MN, 2006. p. 90–91

2005 Levin, Kim, "Voice Choices: 'Paper,' Nicole Klagsbrun Gallery," *The Village Voice*, February 16–22

Johnson, Ken, "Art Listings: Paper," *The New York Times*, February 18.

Vogel, Carol, "Talent Call: Hot New Artists Wanted," *The New York Times*, February 3

2004 Herbert, Martin, "The Office" Art: Preview, *Time Out London*, December 30–January 7

Rosenberg, Karen, "John Pilson," *Frieze*, Issue 80, January

Site Matters, The Lower Manhattan Cultural Council's World Trade Center Artists Residency, 1997–2001

2003 Mclister, Neil, "John Pilson," *ArtForum*, December

Westerbeke, Julia, "John Pilson, 'St. Denis,'" *Time Out New York*, October 30–November 6

Cream 3: Contemporary Art and Culture, Phaidon Press Limited, London, pp. 292–295

Pilson, John. "The Digital Vernacular", *Cabinet*, Issue No. 10, Spring

2001 Huberman, Anthony, "John Pilson" *Loop—Alles auf Anfang, Kunsthalle der Hypo-Kulturstiftung*, Munich, March

Pollack, Barbara, "New York Reviews", *ArtNews*, November
Lerner, Adam, "Moving Pictures", *Artforum*, November (Cover)
The New Yorker, September 24
Anderson, Jeffrey "John Pilson", Venice Biennale Catalogue, Summer
Huberman, Anthony, "Ouverture: John Pilson", *Flash Art*, March–April
Pasquini, Stefano, "The Oxymoron of Venice", *NY Arts*, Summer
Stephanson, Anders, "Openings: John Pilson", *Artforum*, April
Turner, Johnathan and Barbara A. MacAdam, "The Venice Biennale", *ARTnews*, Summer
Williams, Gregory, "Venice Biennale: John Pilson", *Tema Celeste,* Summer
Vetrocq, Marcia E., "Biennale Babylon", *Art in America,* September
2000 Anderson, Jeffrey. P.S. 1 Greater New York Catalogue
Christov-Bakargiev, Carolyn. P.S. 1 *Greater New York* Catalogue
Gopinath, Gabrielle. "Two Critical Comments: Greater New York at P.S. 1," Review NYC, May
Molinari, Guido. *Flash Art* (Italian Edition), Dec. 2000, p.122
The New York Times, City Section, Dec. 31, Romero, Filippo, review, "Shockwave",
Flash Art, Italian Edition, December 2000–January 2001, no. 225
1997 *Double Take Magazine*, December
1994 Aletti, Vince. "Building Dwelling Thinking," *Village Voice*, March

AWARDS

2002 The Bâloise Prize, Art Statements — Art Basel 33, Switzerland

2001 Penny McCall Foundation Award The Young Artists Special Prize, 49th International Exhibition of Art: Plateau of Mankind, Venice Biennale, Italy

2000 Site Matters, The Lower Manhattan Cultural Council's World Trade Center Artists Residency, New York, NY*

Artist-in-Residence, Harvestworks Digital Media Arts Center, NY

1993 John Ferguson Weir Award, Yale University, New Haven, CT

CURATED EXHIBITIONS

2002 *Gravity Over Time*, Erica Baum, Stuart Elster, Maureen Gallace, Wayne Gonzales, An-My Le, Judith Joy Ross, Stephan Shore, 1000 Eventi Gallery, Milan, Italy

1994 *Building, Dwelling, Thinking*, Lowinsky Gallery, NY

PUBLIC COLLECTIONS

Hamburger Kunsthalle, Hamburg, Germany
Stedelijk Museum, Amsterdam, The Netherlands
Fonds National d'Art Contemporain, France
Dallas Museum of Art, Dallas
The Solomon R. Guggenheim Museum, New York
The New York Public Library
The Museum of Modern Art, New York

*Catalogue